IRAQ, MY HANDIWORK

History, Headlines, and Prophecy

SPECIAL EDITION

New York Times Bestselling Author

RON BRACKIN

AND

ISAM GHATTAS

Weller & Bunsby
PUBLISHERS

Published by Weller & Bunsby
wellerandbunsby.com

Italics within all Scripture quotations are the authors'.

ISBN-13: 978-0692246443
ISBN-10: 0692246444

Cover photo: zigazou76
Cover design by Ethan Brackin

To our brothers and sisters in the Iraqi Church, who continue to pay the highest price for their faith, whose vision and call are to bless the earth, and whom "God is not ashamed to be called their God," this little book is affectionately dedicated.

Introduction

To be honest with you, we wrote this book in 2004, about nine months after Coalition troops invaded (or liberated, depending on who tells the story) Iraq. For several reasons that have nothing at all to do with this book, the manuscript has been in a file drawer ever since.

Then, in December 2010, a domino fell in North Africa.

The people of Tunisia took to the streets and drove out President Zine El Abidine Ben Ali. And the whole region exploded.

Demonstrations raged in neighboring Algeria. Jordanians demanded and got the resignation of Prime Minister Samir Rifai. Hosni Mubarak was deposed in Egypt. People rioted in Yemen and Bahrain. Hezbollah seized power in Lebanon. Islamic potentates, one after another, tried to promise, bluff, or bludgeon their way into longer reigns. In Libya, Muammar Gaddafi ordered out his troops and left hundreds dead, outraging the international community and mobilizing the U.N.

Then, on May 1, 2011, President Obama announced to the world that Navy Seals had killed al-Qaeda mass murderer Osama bin Laden.

Clearly, God was moving. Suddenly. Dynamically. Purposefully.

But to what end?

And what should the Church do?

For one thing, we need to change the way we think about Iraq. We need to align ourselves with God and pray and act in accordance with his foreknowledge and plan.

Little has changed in Iraq since 2004. Its issues are the same, its challenges unresolved. American troops are still there. The dinar is still worthless. Sunni, Shi'a, and Kurds are still enemies. And though most of the Iraqi Christians have fled the violence and persecution, many remain—a bold and courageous witness, keepers of the divine trust, and heirs to an ancient promise.

In the following pages, you will walk through Scripture and see a land intertwined with man's destiny and God's plan.

You will meet some of your brothers or sisters—faithful Christians who, while missiles rained down on them in two Gulf wars, shouted desperate prayers of faith with their families and congregations. Who suffered under Saddam's brutal regime. And who now watch in awe as God's hand begins to move in ways they had never dared to dream.

Through it all, you will be given a fresh look at Iraq, not through the eyes of Western media or even through history. You will gaze through the eyes of the ancient prophets. You will look ahead through the ages to the fulfillment of divine promises that will one day affect the whole earth.

about the title

Isaiah 19 is an often-quoted Bible verse among Christians in Egypt and Iraq.

The New International Version of the Bible begins the chapter with the words, "an oracle concerning Egypt." The Amplified Bible renders it more ominously as "the mournful, inspired prediction (a burden to be lifted up) concerning Egypt." And the next seventeen verses could make Egyptians run for the hills.

As with every judgment and chastisement of God, however, light eventually explodes in the darkness. And the prophet begins to speak about a new day in which "there will be an altar to the Lord in the heart of Egypt, and a monument to the Lord at its border. It will be a sign and witness to the Lord Almighty in the land of Egypt."

Verse 21 promises that "the Lord will make himself known to the Egyptians, and in that day they will acknowledge the Lord. They will worship with sacrifices and grain offerings; they will make vows to the Lord and keep them."

The next verse is another downward spike where the Lord sends a plague. But an uptick quickly follows as he answers their prayers and heals them.

So what does this have to do with Iraq?

"In that day there will be a highway from Egypt to Assyria," the prophet says.

Assyria is modern-day Iraq and Syria. We'll set Syria aside for another book. Within these pages, we will substitute the name "Iraq" where Scripture speaks of "Assyria," thereby rendering verses 23-25 as, "The Iraqis will go to Egypt and the Egyptians to Iraq. The Egyptians and the Iraqis will worship together. In that day Israel will be the third, along with Egypt and

Iraq, a blessing on the earth. The Lord Almighty will bless them, saying, 'Blessed be Egypt my people, Iraq my handiwork, and Israel my inheritance."

So the title is God's definition and perception of Iraq. And as such, it needs to become ours.

Chapter One

My (Ron's) part of the story started in January 2004, thirty thousand feet over the warzone known as Iraq.

Isam and the Manara International teams had seen it many times over the past dozen or so years. I had sort of seen it when I was a kid through the eyes of a Vizier's daughter named Scheherazade and more recently through the dusty lenses of FOX News and CNN cameras.

The "Shock and Awe" had stopped nearly ten months earlier. Now, the Iraqi mood was more like "Stress and Angst."

The interim Iraqi government had not yet replaced the Coalition Provisional Authority (CPA). Saddam had recently been found hiding in a "rat hole" and put behind bars, but it would be nearly three years before he would be convicted by an Iraqi Special Tribunal of crimes against humanity and hanged.

Since his capture, attacks by Iraqi resistance against Coalition forces had dropped from forty or fifty a day to about ten or twelve.

It was an interesting experience to land at Saddam International Airport (renamed Baghdad International after it was secured by the U.S. Army's 3rd Infantry Division). All the airspace was military, and our eighteen-seat twin-prop was restricted to a narrow, closely-monitored corridor. Once over the city, we begin a slow spiral down. Suddenly, our port wing tipped up, the starboard wing tipped down, and we dropped about ten thousand feet in a few seconds. Our vital organs were sucked into our shoes. We took a lap, then dropped another ten thousand feet. But it was worth following procedures to avoid being shot out of the sky.

The present incarnation of Iraq was carved out by the British after WWI and the dissolution of the Ottoman Empire. The Arabs expected independence; the League of Nations placed them under a British mandate. Winston Churchill, along with other officials, drew up subjective boundaries which embraced the Kurdish district around Mosul in the north, the Sunni Arab district around Baghdad in the middle, and the Shi'a district in the south around Basra—a volatile formula that virtually guaranteed instability.

The new borders excluded Kuwait, which had been part of the Basra district under the Ottoman Turks. That gambit would backfire after a ruthless young nationalist named Saddam Hussein seized the reins.

For a modern international airport, it was eerily empty. No one else coming in; no one leaving. Just armed security guards, work lights, and echoes.

One of the guards accompanied us onto a shuttle bus, and we snaked our way through concrete barriers and drove to the checkpoint between the airport and Baghdad. Once inside the fenced compound, we were questioned and handed off to Nepalese troops until our van arrived to take us the rest of the way into the city.

Charred Iraqi tanks were still visible along the sides of the road or lying in the sand holes where they had dug in. It was not difficult to imagine what it had been like when our tanks and Humvees thundered into Baghdad back in April.

Just ahead was a crushed, trampled area where a hundred-tank Iraqi barricade had been blasted and burned.

No one shot at us as we drove in, but we knew it could happen at any time. It happened everyday. While resistance attacks against military targets had declined, terrorists attacks against civilian targets were on the rise.

We crossed the ancient Tigris River and entered Baghdad—a far cry from *1,001 Arabian Nights*.

Iraqi National Theatre
(photo source unknown)

Houses dirty and in disrepair. Highways scored by tank treads. Deep, muddy pits were gouged out of side streets. Shops and stores lined the roads. Sidewalks groaned under towers of boxed Western kitchen appliances and home entertainment equipment, creating a bizarre incongruity. Old cars, new cars, bicycles, donkey carts, trucks, mopeds, mangy horses, tractor trailers, and tankers congested the streets and turnabouts. Women dressed crown-to-sole in black chador begged drivers and pedestrians for alms. Gas fumes choked the air.

We passed the towering Media Ministry building and the immense Iraqi National Theatre. Both had been bombed; the former was gutted. Between their charred foundations sat a miracle. A little single-story church, totally untouched. Such was the precision of the bombing—and the power of God's protective hand.

The Communications Tower. Ministry of Trade. Months ago, they appeared all green and flashing, as I watched through the sleepless eyes of the news networks. Now they were gray and smoke-stained and smelled like old campfires.

Baghdad's more than five million people still had no telephone service. Electricity was an on-again/off-again affair, with the emphasis on the latter. Automatic weapons fire popped here and there. Explosions rumbled. They were often close by, but there was no way to tell who was doing what to whom. Thick black smoke filled the sky. It wasn't from one of the refineries, because the refineries were over there and the smoke was over here.

Outside Baghdad, it was worse.

There are only a dozen or so real cities in this country. The rest is desert or broad plains with reedy marshes along the border with Iran and mountains in the north. Despite its history as the fertile Crescent and Cradle of Civilization, only twelve percent of Iraq today is fit for cultivation. In the summer, the heat and sandstorms are suffocating (145° F is not unusual; one GI told me it hit 152°).

Scattered throughout this arid wilderness beyond the cities lives the rural portion of Iraq's twenty-four million souls. Bedouin, with their obedient flocks and black tents, dot the landscape. Here and there, where you least expect it, lies a tiny village that hasn't changed in four centuries.

Mushin Hasan, deputy director of the National Museum of Iraq in Baghdad, sits on destroyed artifacts in April 2003. *Photograph: Mario Tama/Getty*

Estimates vary as to the racial distribution of the Iraqi population. But the CIA put it at about 75-80 percent Arab, 15-20 percent Turkoman, and about 5 percent Assyrian, along with whatever's left over.

Religion breaks out to 97 percent Muslim and 3 percent Christian or "other." The Muslims are further identified as mostly Shi'a and about 35 percent Sunni.

Thanks to three decades of Saddam and a dozen years of sanctions, the Iraqi economy plunged from about $3 to the dinar to around 3,000 dinar to the dollar. Literacy plummeted, too. Only four out of ten Iraqis, sixteen and older, can read and write.

As unfortunate as these statistics are, they are not unique. There are poorer countries. There are people groups farther behind the times. And Iraq is not the only country infested with terrorists.

So why this book about Iraq? What makes this little Middle Eastern country so special? Two things.

Iraq's past.

Iraq's future.

Sadly, some of the greatest records of its past were stolen and destroyed by looters during the initial days of Operation Iraqi Freedom. Robert Fisk, Middle East Correspondent for the Independent of London mourned its loss as he walked through the rubble of Iraq's National Archaeological Museum:

> They lie across the floor in tens of thousands of pieces, the priceless antiquities of Iraq's history. The looters had gone from shelf to shelf, systematically pulling down the statues and pots and amphorae of the Assyrians and the Babylonians, the Sumerians, the Medes, the Persians and the Greeks and hurling them onto the concrete.
>
> A glass case that had once held 40,000-year-old stone and flint objects had been smashed open. It lay empty. No one knows what

> happened to the Assyrian reliefs from the royal palace of Khorsabad, nor the 5000-year-old gold leaf earrings once buried with Sumerian princesses. It will take decades to sort through what they have left, the broken stone torsos, the tomb treasures, the bits of jewelry glinting amid the piles of smashed pots.
>
> Only a few weeks ago, Jabir Khalil Ibrahim, the director of Iraq's State Board of Antiquities, referred to the museum's contents as "the heritage of the nation." They were, he said, "not just things to see and enjoy. We get strength from them to look to the future."[1]

Though many of the ancient artifacts were lost, an amazing amount of Iraq's history is preserved forever and indestructible on the pages of Scripture.

Countless chapters of Christian history—as well as the history of mankind—are written here. Iraq is the codifier of law, disseminator of languages, founder of agriculture, and birthplace of written communication. It is also the country mentioned most frequently in the Bible, save for Israel.

[1] Robert Fisk, "A Civilization Torn to Pieces," *Independent* Digital (UK) Ltd, Sunday, April 13, 2003.

You won't find the word "Iraq" in any concordance. Theories concerning the term's etymology vary, several of the most popular being that a) it comes from biblical Erech, b) it is an Arabic term for the geographical area in the south-central portion of the country, or c) it is a modern spelling of Urek, an ancient Sumerian city state.

To find Iraq in the Bible, you must play detective and look for it under its aliases: Mesopotamia, the land of Shinar, Assyria, Babylon, Ur of the Chaldeans, Tigris, Euphrates, and Nineveh. You must search for clues in Genesis, Kings, and Chronicles, Ezra and Nehemiah, Isaiah, Jeremiah and Ezekiel, Jonah, Acts, Peter's letters, and John's revelatory vision. After a while, it will seem as though you can hardly turn a page of Scripture without running smack into Iraq … and cringe as you read yet another account of its rebellious and bloody history.

But God has not abandoned Iraq, for all of its evil, cruelty, and violence. He has used it in the past to accomplish his will, and today's Iraqi Church is convinced that he will use it again.

We begin at the beginning—the very beginning…

Chapter Two

History begins with God. It is, says the old saw, "his-story." The story of God's relationship, or lack of relationship, with his creation.

"In the beginning, God created the heavens and the earth."[2]

Moses continues in chapter two to explain that "the Lord God had planted a garden in the east, in Eden; and there he put the man he had formed. And the Lord God made all kinds of trees grow out of the ground—trees that were pleasing to the eye and good for food. In the middle of the garden were the tree of life and the tree of the knowledge of good and evil."

Just where was this awesome garden? Scripture provides us with a few tantalizing clues.

"A river watering the garden flowed from Eden' from there it was separated into four headwaters. The name of the first is the Pishon; it winds through the entire land of Havilah, where there is gold. (The gold of that land is good; aromatic resin [bdellium] and onyx are also there.) The name of the second river is the Gihon; it winds through the entire land of Cush. The name of the third river is the Tigris; it runs along the east side of Asshur. And the fourth river is the Euphrates."[3]

So far, so good.

---

[2] Genesis 1:1.
[3] Genesis 2:10-14.

Merrill Unger explains that the Pishon and the Gihon "were presumably canals (called 'rivers' in Babylonia) which connected the Tigris and Euphrates as ancient river beds. Some scholars identify it with the Pallakottos Canal near the ancient Sumerian town of Eridu, not far from Abraham's city of Ur" in southern Iraq.[4]

Others, however, theorize that Eden was farther north, in Turkey. Still other scholars place it in Mongolia, India, or Ethiopia (ancient Cush), in the belief that the Pishon and the Gihon were actually the Nile and the Ganges rivers.

Another Eden hunter is Dr. Juris Zarins of Southwest Missouri State University. Armed with an arsenal of scientific and historical disciplines, Zarins places Eden at the bottom of the Gulf. One stone of his evidential foundation is a LANDSAT image that reveals a fossil river buried deep beneath the sand which flowed through a couple of dry beds known today as the Wadi Riniah and the Wadi Batin.

Citing the biblical account, Dora Jane Hamblin writes: "this region was rich in bdellium, an aromatic gum resin that can still be found in north Arabia, and gold, which was still mined in the general area in the 1950s."[5]

Speculation over the centuries, however, has focused only on *where* Eden might have been. No one has questioned its *size*.

---

[4] Merrill F. Unger, *Unger's Bible Dictionary* (Moody Press, Chicago), 1985, Pearl C. Unger, Third Edition, p. 868.

[5] Dora Jane Hamblin, "Has the Garden of Eden been located at last?" *Smithsonian Magazine*, Volume 18, No. 2, May 1987.

It may help us to remember that, in addition to creating Adam, the Lord God "had formed out of the ground all of the beasts of the field and all the birds of the air" and "brought them to the man to see what he would name them; and whatever the man called each living creature, that was its name. So the man gave names to all the livestock, the birds of the air and all the beasts of the field."[6]

If we believe in the accuracy of the Genesis account of creation, rather than Darwinian Evolution or other theories, we are confronted with a host of critters—one of each gender—that would have occupied a vast and climatically diverse piece of real estate. Could it be, then, that all of the Eden theorists are correct, including Dr. Zarins? Could the Garden of Eden have covered Iraq *and* Egypt *and* Turkey and Ethiopia *and* India *and* Mongolia, and even more?

Regardless, since Iraq is demonstrably what is referred to as Mesopotamia, the Fertile Crescent, and the Cradle of Civilization and, since Eden was by biblical account God's personal garden and therefore the most fertile and productive land imaginable, it is likely that at least part of Eden was in Iraq (modern tour agencies are quick to confirm this. One guide recently recommended that I visit "Qurna, where the Tigris meets the Euphrates. Qurna is said to be the site of the biblical Garden of Eden, where you can find Adam's tree of the

[6] Genesis 1:19-20.

knowledge of good and evil." Did I really look that gullible?).

Extending the postulation, we can say that Cain and Abel might well have been among the first Iraqis. But even if they were not, their lives provide a graphic portrait of the region's history.

Cain, the bloody son. Abel, the son who pleased God.

Iraq has always been inhabited by men of blood—from Cain to Hussein—alongside those who pleased God. After the first murder, Seth "had a son, and he named him Enosh. At that time men began to call on the name of the Lord."[7]

Not all, however, called on the Lord's name. Many drifted farther and farther away from him and became intolerably corrupt, until man's wickedness became so great "that every inclination of the thoughts of his heart was only evil all the time," and "the Lord was grieved that he had made man on the earth."[8]

Like tears of grief flowing from the Throne, the heavens opened, and a great global flood thundered across the globe, wiping the slate clean and giving the earth a new beginning.

---

[7] Genesis 4:26.

[8] Genesis 6:5-6.

Chapter Three

God started fresh with Noah's family—his good wife, their sons, Shem, Ham, and Japheth, and their sons' spouses. Eight people, judged by God to be righteous. These eight grew into clans and the clans into nations.

The Genesis account continues to describe a world that "had one language and a common speech. As men moved eastward, they found a plain in Shinar and settled there."[9]

The plain of Shinar is in southern Iraq where, in Genesis 10, we are introduced to a very ambitious and talented man named Nimrod.

The account explains that "the first centers of his kingdom were Babylon, Erech, Akkad and Calneh, in Shinar."[10] A quick geography lesson places ancient Erech on the left bank of the Euphrates, about one hundred miles southeast of Babylon. Akkad was on the Euphrates, just southwest of modern Baghdad. No one is certain just where Calneh was, but Scripture places it in the same general area.

Here in southern Iraq, then, a terrible rebellion broke out against God. And to this day, you and I suffer its extraordinary consequences.

> "Come," said the ungrateful descendants of Noah, "let us build ourselves a city, with a tower that

---

[9] Genesis 11:1.
[10] Genesis 10:10.

> reaches to the heavens, so that we may make a name for ourselves and not be scattered over the face of the whole earth.
>
> But the Lord came down to see the city and the tower that the men were building. The Lord said, "If as one people speaking the same language they have begun to do this, then nothing they plan to do will be impossible for them. Come let us go down and confuse their language so they will not understand each other."
>
> So the Lord scattered them from there over all the earth, and they stopped building the city. That is why it was called Babel—because there the Lord confused the language of the whole world.[11]

Today, we take great pains to learn foreign languages in order to communicate with people of other nations or tribes. The confusion of languages resulting from that historic rebellion in Iraq continues to facilitate discord and disunity among people groups and impede the spreading of the Gospel.

Unfortunately, that same rebellious spirit continues to rule over Iraq. We have heard its hoarse echo up the millennial corridors and out

---

[11] Genesis 11:4-9.

of the mouth of Saddam Hussein, who isolated Iraq from the rest of the world. Who punished any Iraqi suspected of opposing him with prison, torture, and/or death. Who identified himself with Joseph Stalin and Nebuchadnezzar, and Saladin. Who sacrificed anyone or anything in order to make a name for himself.

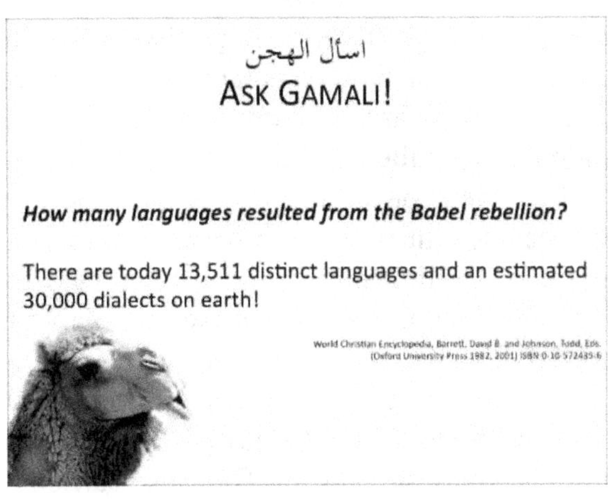

✠

Genesis 12 continues in Iraq, in a city known as Ur of the Chaldeans, where we meet a man of nearly inconceivable faith.

Stepping back one chapter, we find the account of Noah's son, Shem. One of Shem's descendants was named Nahor. When Nahor was twenty-nine years old, he became the father of Terah who, as a septuagenarian, fathered Abram, Nahor, and Haran. Haran was born in Ur, sired Lot, Milcah, and Iscah, and died in Ur. All we are told about this second Nahor is that he seems to have married his niece, Milcah. 'Nuff said.

Abram married a woman named Sarai, and around 2100 B.C., they left Ur in southern Iraq to go to Canaan in what is now Israel. They got as far as Haran in modern Turkey, on the Belikh River, sixty miles from where it emptied into the Euphrates. Abram and his wife settled there for a while and then moved on to Canaan.

There, the happy couple became rich and grew into a huge tribe, so huge that he and his nephew, Lot, had to separate. Abram stayed where he was, and Lot chose to move to an infamous city called Sodom.

Life went on until Genesis 14, where we find the account of a battle between four kings (of Elam, Goiim, Shinar, and Ellasar) and five kings (of Sodom, Gomorrah, Admah, Zeboiim, and Bela/Zoar).

The four beat the five and "seized all the goods of Sodom and Gomorrah and all their food; then they went away. They also carried off Abram's nephew Lot and his possessions, since he was living in Sodom."[12]

But Lot was kin, so Abram marshaled three hundred eighteen fighting men out of his vast household and went after the four kings, beating them and recovering the booty and captives, including Lot and his household.

Of interest to our purposes is that two of the four kings were Iraqis—Arioch, King of Ellasar, and Kedorlaomer, King of Elam. Ellasar was a chief city of Babylonia, serving as the center of worship of the sun (Shamash) in the south. Elam was a powerful and aggressive city in lower

---

[12] Genesis 14:11-12.

Babylonia and a frequent thorn in Assyria's side.

Iraq appears once more in the first book of the Bible.[13] Among the listed kings of Edom, we meet "Shaul from Rehoboth on the river." Rehoboth was in Iraq. Therefore, an Iraqi once ruled over Edom (Idumaea, south of the Dead Sea in modern-day Jordan).

From Abram and Shaul, we fast forward—past Egypt and the Exodus, past Joshua and the Judges, past David and Solomon and the divided kingdoms of Israel and Judah—to a cruel and bloody group of northern Iraqis.

[13] Genesis 36: 37 (repeated in 1 Chronicles 1:48).

Chapter Four

Throughout the period of the divided kingdom of Israel, most nations "were looters, building their state by robbing other nations. Assyria was the most ferocious of them all. Its very name became a byword for cruelty and atrocity. They skinned their prisoners alive and cut off various body parts to inspire terror to their enemies. There are records of Assyrian officials pulling out tongues and displaying mounds of human skulls—all to bring about stark horror and wealthy tribute from surrounding nations. Nowhere are the pages of history more bloody than in the records of their ward."[14]

Despite this history, sometime in the early eighth century B.C.—during the last years of the reign of Adad-Nirari III and Semiramis, the queen regent, or the early reign of Assurdan III—God dispatched an Israeli prophet named Jonah to preach a revival in Assyria.

Mighty Nineveh on the eastern bank of the Tigris River in northern Iraq, was one of the many cities founded by Nimrod. Sargon II later established Nineveh as the capital of the Assyrian Empire. Its ruins today—a perimeter of grassy mounds, interrupted by several massive gates and brief stretches of the original walls—lie in the modern city of Mosul. The mounds cover the remains of magnificent temples, palaces, and fortifications, an eerie confirmation of God's words against Nineveh

---

[14] http://www.bible-history.com/oldtestament/BKA2The_Assyrians.htm.

through the prophet Nahum: "I will prepare your grave, for you are vile."[15]

But God was willing to forgive Nineveh, if it would repent. Jonah, however, was all too familiar with its ruthless citizens. He knew that Nineveh was a "city of blood, full of lies, full of plunder, never without victims! The crack of whips, the clatter of wheels, galloping horses and jolting chariots! Charging cavalry, flashing swords and glittering spears! Many casualties, piles of dead, bodies without number, people stumbling over the corpses …"[16]

Instead of pining for its redemption, Jonah longed to see the Assyrians get what was coming to them at the relentless hands of an angry God.

The biblical book that bears his name tells the brief but instructive story of the prophet's attempt to flee from the Lord, his three-day incarceration in the belly of a great fish, and his tardy and reluctant obedience.

It also testifies to one of history's most unlikely revivals.

Jonah preached an eight-word message, door-to-door and street-to-street, throughout the city. One of the shortest sermons in history. Just one sentence: "Forty more days and Nineveh will be overturned." While he may have had more to say, Scripture records only the penetrating punch line.

When they heard that sentence, the Assyrians "declared a fast, and all of them, from

---

[15] Nahum 1:14.
[16] Nahum 3:1-3.

the greatest to the least, put on sackcloth. When the news reached the king of Nineveh, he rose from his throne, took off his royal robes, covered himself with sackcloth and sat down in the dust.

> Then he issued a proclamation in Nineveh: "By the decree of the king and his nobles: Do not let any man or beast, herd or flock, taste anything; do not let them eat or drink. But let man and beast be covered with sackcloth. Let everyone call urgently on God. Let them give up their evil ways and their violence. Who knows? God may yet relent and with compassion turn from his fierce anger so that we will not perish.[17]

And God did.

What a revival! Even the livestock took part!

Unfortunately, the Assyrians relapsed into their evil ways and their violence, and the capital was ravaged about one hundred fifty years later.

Fast forward again to 2 Kings 15:17. Assyria is expanding its empire and setting its sights on a reprobate Israel.

Menahem was King of Israel in Samaria and reigned for ten years. This was not a good time for the divided kingdom. Both Israel and

---

[17] Jonah 3.

Judah were drifting away from the Lord, so far so that judgment was inevitable.

During Menahem's reign, Pul—aka Tiglath-pileser III, king of Assyria—invaded the land. Menahem bought him off temporarily with a thousand talents (about thirty-seven tons) of silver.[18] Menahem's son, Pekahiah, succeeded his father, but he was assassinated a couple years later. Then Pekah, one of his chief officers (oddly enough, also one of the assassins) took the throne.

During Pekah's reign, Iraqi king Tiglath-pileser was busy expanding his kingdom. In one sweep along the Mediterranean, he captured more than half a dozen towns in Palestine and carried off their citizens to Assyria.

After sixteen years on the throne, Pekah joined forces with the Aramaic kingdom in Syria and attacked his brothers in Judah. King Ahaz of Judah retaliated by calling to Tiglath-pileser for help. To sweeten the spoils, Ahaz looted the royal palace and the Lord's temple and gave Tiglath-pileser a pile of silver and gold. The Assyrian king accepted the gift and sacked Damascus, deporting the Syrian survivors and killing its king.[19] Three years later, Pekah was assassinated, proving once again that what goes around comes around.

Hoshea was the next—and last—king of Israel.

Hoshea had been vassal to Assyria/Iraq, which was now ruled by Shalmaneser IV. To keep Assyria from destroying Israel, Hoshea

---

[18] 2 Kings 15:19-20.

[19] 2 Kings 16.

paid tribute. But Hoshea betrayed the king, and Shalmaneser learned that Hoshea had stopped payment on his checks and was plotting against him with Egypt, Assyria's historical foe.

"Therefore Shalmaneser seized him and put him in prison … marched against Samaria and laid siege to it for three years."[20]

"Sieges are hard work for both sides, and ancient sieges were particularly arduous," explains John D. Beatty. "Disease and starvation are endemic to both sides, even during modern sieges." He goes on to describe the additional "weakening effects of long-term short rations."

"Fresh food acquisition and waste disposal has always been a problem in sieges, and in ancient sieges was often decisive." As a result of all the horrible deaths from disease and starvation, there were "mass cremations" and "the stench of death and burning flesh."[21]

Chronicling an earlier siege of Samaria by Ben-Hadad, the Aramean king, the Bible describes "a great famine in the city; the siege lasted so long that a donkey's head sold for eighty shekels [two pounds] of silver, and a quarter of a cab [one-half pint] of seed pods [or dove's dung] for five shekels [about two ounces]."[22]

At one point during the siege, the king of Israel was called upon to settle a grisly dispute. One mother had proposed to another that she

---

[20] 2 Kings 17:4-5.
[21] John D. Beatty, "A Different Horse: Alternate Interpretations of the Trojan War."
[22] 2 Kings 6:25.

give up her “son so we may eat him today, and tomorrow we’ll eat my son.”

“So we cooked my son and ate him,” explained the second mother to the king. “The next day I said to her, ‘Give up your son so we may eat him,’ but she had him hidden.”[23]

Though the Lord miraculously lifted this siege, Israel failed to learn its lesson, leaving the Lord no alternative but to send another siege, this one at the hands of the fierce Iraqis. And this next time, the Lord would turn away his face from his people, and his ear would be deaf to their cries.

“In the ninth year of Hoshea, the king of Assyria captured Samaria and deported the Israelites [the ten tribes] to Assyria. He settled

[23] 2 Kings 6:28-29.

them in Halah, in Gozan on the Habor River and in the town of the Medes."[24]

Thus ended the northern kingdom of Israel forever. But it was not the end of God's people, for there will be a time when God will "reclaim the remnant that is left of his people from Assyria, from Lower Egypt, from Upper Egypt, from Cush, from Elam, from Babylon, from Hamath and from the islands of the sea."[25]

In short, "a shoot will come up from the stump of Jesse; from his roots a Branch will bear fruit. The Spirit of the Lord will rest on him—the Spirit of wisdom and of understanding, the Spirit of counsel and of power, the Spirit of knowledge and of the fear of the Lord—and he will delight in the fear of the Lord."[26]

Though the Lord used Assyria to judge Israel, it was far from guiltless. And these ancient Iraqis had no idea that they were being used as the Lord's instrument of correction. They thought conquering Israel was all their doing and for their own ends.

> Woe to the Assyrian, the rod of my anger, in whose hand is the club of my wrath! I send him against a godless nation, I dispatch him against a people who anger me, to seize loot and snatch plunder, and to trample them down like mud in the

---

[24] 2 Kings 17:4-6.
[25] Isaiah 11:11.
[26] Isaiah 11:1-3.

> streets. But this is not what he intends, this is not what he has in mind; his purpose is to destroy, to put an end to many nations."[27]

Now that God had finished wielding Assyria, he would soon take up another sword—this time from southern Iraq—to cut Assyria to pieces.

> I will punish the king of Assyria for the willful pride of his heart and the haughty look in his eyes. For he says: "By the strength of my hand I have done this" … Therefore, the Lord, the Lord Almighty, will send a wasting disease upon his sturdy warriors; under his pomp a fire will be kindled like a blazing flame.… In that day, the remnant of Israel, the survivors of the house of Jacob, will no longer rely on him who struck them down but will truly rely on the Lord, the Holy One of Israel. A remnant will return, a remnant of Jacob will return to the Mighty God.…
>
> Therefore, this is what the Lord, the Lord Almighty, says: "O my people who live in Zion, do not be afraid of the Assyrians, who beat you with a rod and lift up a club against you, as

---

[27] Isaiah 10:5-7.

> Egypt did. Very soon my anger against you will end and my wrath will be directed to their destruction.[28]

اسأل الهجن

ASK GAMALI!

What did the Jews of Jesus' time have against Samaritans?

It was linked to Iraq. After the Assyrian king deported the Jews from Israel to Assyria, he "brought people from Babylon, Cuthah, Avva, Hamath and Sepharvaim and settled them in the towns of Samaria to replace the Israelites." But they were not Jews and didn't worship the Lord. So the Lord sent lions to eat them up. When Sargon II heard this, he sent back one of the priests who had been taken captive to teach the settlers how to worship the Lord. They learned, but they didn't give up their own idols. And they continued trying to serve both the Lord and their idols for centuries.

2 Kings 17:24-41

Sargon II was succeeded by Sennacherib, who ruled Assyria from 705 to 681 B.C.

Israel and its ten northern tribes were now in captivity in Assyria. No trace of these tribes was ever seen again—although there are many myths and traditions claiming to have found evidence of them, primarily in Africa, and the prophet Micah seems to suggest that God preserved a remnant among the exiles who would serve as his witness as they were dispersed through the nations:

---

[28] Isaiah 10:12-13, 15, 16, 20-21, 24-25.

> "The remnant of Jacob will be in the midst of many peoples like dew from the Lord, like showers on the grass, which do not wait for man or linger for mankind."[29]

Its blood still hot from recent conquest, Assyria turned its eye on the remaining two tribes in Judah.

Hezekiah had been king of Judah for fourteen years when Sennacherib laid siege against its fortified cities.

> When Hezekiah saw that Sennacherib had come and that he intended to make war on Jerusalem, he … blocked all the springs and the stream that flowed through the land. "Why should the kings of Assyria come and find plenty of water?" they said. Then he worked hard repairing all the broken sections of the wall and building towers on it. He built another wall outside that one and reinforced the supporting terraces of the City of David. He also made large numbers of weapons and shields. He appointed military officers over the people and assembled them before him in the square at the city gate and encouraged them with these words: "Be strong and courageous. Do not

[29] Micah 5:7.

> be afraid or discouraged because of the king of Assyria and the vast army with him, for there is a greater power with us than with him. With him is only the arm of flesh, but with us is the Lord our God to help us and to fight our battles." And the people gained confidence from what Hezekiah the king of Judah said.[30]

But Hezekiah tried to hedge his bet by attempting to buy off the Assyrian king for eleven tons of silver and about a ton of gold—which, like Ahaz before him, he looted from the palace treasuries and the temple of the Lord.[31]

Sennacherib, however, was one savvy Iraqi. He knew he would have gotten all the gold and silver anyway, so he sent his field commander to talk Hezekiah into surrendering. But the Babylonian officers, in their boasting and taunting of Hezekiah and the Lord, did themselves more harm than good.

Instead of being intimidated, Hezekiah and his officials put on sackcloth and cried out to God:

> "O Lord Almighty, God of Israel, enthroned between the cherubim, you alone are God over all the kingdoms of the earth. You have made heaven and earth. Give ear, O Lord, and hear; open your eyes, O

---

[30] 2 Chronicles 32:4-8.

[31] 2 Kings 18.

> Lord, and see; listen to all the words Sennacherib has sent to insult the living God. It is true, O Lord, that the Assyrian kings have laid waste all these peoples and their lands. They have thrown their gods into the fire and destroyed them, for they were not gods but only wood and stone, fashioned by human hands. Now, O Lord our God, deliver us from his hand, so that all kingdoms on earth may know that you alone, O Lord, are God."[32]

Through Isaiah, God assured them that he would fight for Judah.

> That night the angel of the Lord went out and put to death a hundred and eighty-five thousand men in the Assyrian camp. When the people got up the next morning—there were all the dead bodies! So Sennacherib king of Assyria broke camp and withdrew. He returned to Nineveh and stayed there.
>
> One day, while he was worshiping in the temple of his god Nisroch, his sons Adrammelech and Sharezer cut him down with the sword, and they escaped to the land of Ararat. And

[32] Isaiah 37:16-20.

> Esarhaddon his son succeeded him as king.[33]

This took place in 682 B.C., yet Iraq's bloody history continued.

---

[33] 2 Kings 19:35-37.

Chapter Five

The feud between Babylon and Assyria was long and bitter.

Finally, in the seventh century B.C., Babylon, under Nabopolassar (Nebuchadnezzar's father), formed an alliance with the Medes, who were ruled by Cyaxares (who became Nebuchadnezzar's father-in-law through an arranged marriage to his daughter, Amyitis). And their armies laid a horrifying two-month siege against Nineveh.

The city fell during the summer of 612. Its demise is described graphically by the prophet Nahum (who sixteenth-century historians believed to have been born at Alkosh, near Mosul—which, interestingly, would have made this prophet an Iraqi).

Nahum predicted that a key to the city's destruction would be "an overwhelming flood" through which the Lord "will make an end of Nineveh; he will pursue his foes into darkness." [34] And history confirms that the "great victory was due in part to the releasing of the city's water supply and the inundation of the Koser River, dissolving the sun-dried brick of which much of the city was built."[35]

Like a journalist embedded with Babylonian troops, the prophet offers one of the most graphic, detailed, and terrifying descriptions in the Bible:

---

[34] Nahum 1:8.

[35] Idem, Merrill F. Unger, p. 796.

An attacker advances against you, Nineveh. Guard the fortress, watch the road, brace yourselves, marshal all your strength! The shields of his soldiers are red; the warriors are clad in scarlet. The metal on the chariots flashes on the day they are made ready; the spears of pine are brandished. The chariots storm through the streets, rushing back and forth through the squares. They look like flaming torches; they dart about like lightning.

He summons his picked troops, yet they stumble on their way. They dash to the city wall; the protective shield is put in place. The river gates are thrown open and the palace collapses. It is decreed that the city be exiled and carried away. Its slave girls moan like doves and beat upon their breasts. Nineveh is like a pool, and its water is draining away.

"Stop! Stop!" they cry, but no one turns back.

Plunder the silver! Plunder the gold! The supply is endless, the wealth from all its treasures! She is pillaged, plundered, stripped! Hearts melt, knees give way, bodies tremble, every face grows pale....

> Look at your troops—they are all women! the gates of your land are wide open to your enemies; fire has consumed their bars.
>
> Draw water for the siege, strengthen your defenses! Work the clay, tread the mortar, repair the brickwork! There the fire will devour you; the sword will cut you down and, like grasshoppers, consume you....
>
> O king of Assyria, your shepherds slumber; your nobles lie down to rest. Your people are scattered on the mountains with no one to gather them. Nothing can heal your wound; your injury is fatal. Everyone who hears the news about you claps his hands at your fall, for who has not felt your endless cruelty?[36]

The city's destruction was so complete that historians long after wondered whether Nineveh was really just a myth.

To understand God's plan for Iraq, we do well to remember that, while he used the Iraqis to chastise the people of the covenant, he brought the people of the covenant into the bosom of Iraq with a heart toward its redemption.

Israel was rebellious, idolatrous, and ripe

[36] Nahum 2:1-10; 3:13-15, 18-19.

for judgment. But among the exiles was a remnant that was faithful to the Lord.

And as we turn our attention to the south, we encounter yet another of God's remnants.

اسأل الهجن

Ask Gamali!

How do we know that Nineveh really existed?

During his reign, Assyrian King Sennacherib surrounded the inner city with a massive wall eight miles long and about 50 feet high. While excavating the ruins, Austen Layard discovered the king's 71-room palace, its walls lined with magnificent sculptured stone slabs, many of which can be seen today in The British Museum. In addition to the palace, the Kuyunjik Mound held the library of Ashurbanipal – 22,000 clay tablets that have provided invaluable historical information on Old Testament life and events.

Merrill F. Unger, Unger's Bible Dictionary (Moody Press, Chicago) Third Edition, p.796

Chapter Six

The stage is set. Hezekiah is king of Judah, the other half of the kingdom that split during Solomon's reign. Unlike most of his predecessors, Hezekiah is described as a man who "did what was right in the eyes of the Lord, just as his father David had done."[37]

As we pick up the account, we find Hezekiah ill and dying. The king pleads with God, and the Lord gives him fifteen more years to live.

Meanwhile, back in Iraq, Baladan is king of Babylon. Hearing of Hezekiah's illness and recovery, he sends Hezekiah a greeting card and a gift. Hezekiah is pleased with this gesture and gives Baladan's envoys the royal tour, carelessly revealing both his defenses and his treasures—not the brightest coin in the pouch, as Isaiah is faithful to point out. But the sword will not fall during Hezekiah's lifetime, and that is all that concerns this king.

Hezekiah's successor, Manasseh, will prove to be one of the most wicked kings since Ahab.

> He rebuilt the high places his father Hezekiah had destroyed; he also erected altars to Baal and made an Asherah pole, as Ahab king of Israel had done. He bowed down to all the starry hosts and worshiped them. He built altars in the temple of the Lord, of which the Lord had said, "In

---

[37] 2 Kings 18:3.

> Jerusalem I will put my Name." In both courts of the temple of the Lord, he built altars to all the starry hosts. He sacrificed his own son in the fire, practiced sorcery and divination, and consulted mediums and spiritists. He did much evil in the eyes of the Lord, provoking him to anger.[38]

God responded by promising "to bring such disaster on Jerusalem and Judah that the ears of everyone who hears of it will tingle. I will stretch out over Jerusalem the measuring line used against Samaria and the plumb line used against the house of Ahab. I will wipe out Jerusalem as one wipes a dish, wiping it and turning it upside down. I will forsake the remnant of my inheritance and hand them over to their enemies. They will be looted and plundered by all their foes, because they have done evil in my eyes and have provoked me to anger from the day their forefathers came out of Egypt until this day. Moreover, Manasseh also shed so much innocent blood that he filled Jerusalem from end to end…"[39]

As with Hezekiah, the promised punishment did not fall on Manasseh, although Judah was invaded by the Assyrian army, "who took Manasseh prisoner, put a hook in his nose, bound him with bronze shackles and took him to Babylon."[40]

---

[38] 2 Kings 21:3-6.

[39] 2 Kings 21:12-16.

[40] 2 Chronicles 33:11.

Manasseh, however, repented during his stay in Iraq, and God "brought him back to Jerusalem and to his kingdom. Then Manasseh knew that the Lord is God" and, once returned to power, he tried to undo all the evil that he had done.[41]

So the Lord held back the sword of Iraq yet a little longer.

Succeeding Manasseh, Amon ruled Judah and continued the evil work of his father.

But no sword.

Josiah, the boy king, was only eight years old when he ascended the throne of Judah. He was a good boy who "did what was right in the eyes of the Lord and walked in all the ways of his father David, not turning aside to the right or to the left."[42] Josiah reigned for thirty-one years and still no sword.

Jehoiakim was next. Another stinker. He lasted eleven years, and finally the ring of the sword could be heard as it slid from its sheath.

But Judah would not be paying for the sins of Jehoiakim or even for the multiplied sins of his successor, Nebuchadnezzar.

Judah will be destroyed "because of the sins of Manasseh and all he had done, including the shedding of innocent blood. For he had filled Jerusalem with innocent blood, and the Lord was not willing to forgive."[43]

Surely, these are among the most terrifying words in Scripture—*the Lord was not willing to forgive.*

---

[41] 2 Chronicles 33:12-16.

[42] 2 Chronicles 34:1-2.

[43] 2 Kings 24:3-4.

"Even if Moses and Samuel were to stand before me," the Lord told Jeremiah, "my heart would not go out to this people. Send them away from my presence! Let them go! And if they ask you, 'Where shall we go?' tell them, "This is what the Lord says: 'Those destined for death, to death; those for the sword, to the sword; those for starvation, to starvation; those for captivity, to captivity.' I will send four kinds of destroyers against them, declares the Lord, the sword to kill and the dogs to drag away and the birds of the air and the beasts of the earth to devour and destroy. I will make them abhorrent to all the kingdoms of the earth because of what Manasseh son of Hezekiah king of Judah did in Jerusalem."[44]

But Manasseh repented, you might argue. And Josiah was a godly man, like David.

"Nevertheless, the Lord did not turn away from the heat of his fierce anger, which burned against Judah because of all that Manasseh had done to provoke him to anger."[45]

Does this mean that there is a sin so grievous that God cannot or will not forgive it?

No.

The Hebrew word, *calach*, sometimes translated as "to forgive" also means "to pardon" or "to spare." A pardon is the remission of the penalty, the release of the obligation of

the offender to bear the displeasure of the offended party. God had decided that Judah would suffer the penalty of his displeasure. He

[44] Jeremiah 15:1-4.

[45] 2 Kings 23:26.

was unwilling to remit that penalty or to spare them the suffering.

He does that with his children today as well.

A man can quit smoking and repent of damaging the body God blessed him with and be forgiven. But, apart from a healing miracle, his lungs have been permanently damaged, and he may still die of agonizing lung cancer or emphysema. Likewise, a man may murder, repent, and receive forgiveness from God and even the family of his victim. Yet, he may still be executed.

Judah's judgment, therefore, should give pause to nations today whose people shed the innocent blood of children out of greed, fear, lust, or convenience. For God declares, "I the Lord do not change."[46]

In 597 B.C., Nebuchadnezzar, one of the most famous Iraqi kings, invaded Judah and made Jehoiakim his vassal. Jehoiakim paid tribute for three years. Then Jehoiakim rebelled.

"The Lord sent Babylonian, Aramean, Moabite and Ammonite raiders against him. He sent them to destroy Judah in accordance with the word of the Lord proclaimed by his servants the prophets."[47]

But this was not yet the end.

Nebuchadnezzar captured Jehoiakim, bound him with bronze shackles, and took him to Babylon. Jehoiakim was succeeded by Jehoiachin—a teenager who walked in his father's errant footsteps, which seems

---

[46] Malachi 3:6.
[47] Isaiah 24:2.

remarkable with the savage Babylonian army camped at his doorstep—a motivation for reconciliation with God if ever there was one.

Iraqi King Nebuchadnezzar laid siege to Jerusalem. And after only three months in office, Jehoiachin surrendered.

> In 587 B.C., Nebuchadnezzar removed all the treasures from the temple of the Lord and from the royal palace and took away all the gold articles that Solomon king of Israel had made for the temple of the Lord. He carried into exile all Jerusalem: all the officers and fighting men, and all the craftsmen and artisans—a total of ten thousand. Only the poorest people of the land were left.
>
> Nebuchadnezzar took Jehoiachin captive to Babylon. He also took from Jerusalem to Babylon the king's mother, his wives, his officials and the leading men of the land. The king of Babylon also deported to Babylon the entire force of seven thousand fighting men, strong and fit for war and one thousand craftsmen and artisans. He made Mattaniah, Jehoiachin's uncle, king in his place and changed his name to Zedekiah."[48]

---

[48] 2 Kings 24:13-17.

But Nebuchadnezzar wasn't finished quite yet.

Separation from God always causes people to do stupid things because, in place of the Lord's guidance, we have nothing to rely on but our own ideas.

So Zedekiah—aka Mattaniah, Jehoiachin's uncle—who had been left in charge, rebelled against Nebuchadnezzar.

As might be expected, the Iraqi king assembled his troops, marched back to Jerusalem, and laid another siege.

Zedekiah sent men to Jeremiah to inquire of the Lord. "Perhaps the Lord will perform wonders for us as in times past so that he [Nebuchadnezzar] will withdraw from us."[49]

But the Lord said no.

More precisely, the Lord said, "I am about to turn against you the weapons of war that are in your hands, which you are using to fight the king of Babylon and the Babylonians who are outside the wall besieging you. And I will gather them inside this city. I myself will fight against you with an outstretched hand and a mighty arm in anger and fury and great wrath. I will strike down those who live in this city—both men and animals—and they will die of a terrible plague. After that, declares the Lord, I will hand over Zedekiah king of Judah, his officials and the people in this city who survive the plague, sword and famine, to Nebuchadnezzar king of Babylon and to their

---

[49] Jeremiah 21:2.

enemies who seek their lives. He will put them to the sword; he will show them no mercy or pity or compassion."[50]

After more than a year and a half, the famine was excruciating. The Babylonians broke through the city wall, and Zedekiah and his army fled. But the Iraqi army overran them in the plains of Jericho, scattered Judah's army, and captured the king. Zedekiah was taken to Nebuchadnezzar.

"They killed the sons of Zedekiah before his eyes. Then they put out his eyes, bound him with bronze shackles and took him to Babylon."[51]

Eleven years after he had sacked Jerusalem, Nebuchadnezzar finished the job. What he had left behind in the Temple before, he now carried off.

The Babylonians "killed their young men with the sword in the sanctuary, and spared neither young man nor young woman, old man or aged. God handed all of them over to Nebuchadnezzar."[52]

His army burned down the Temple, the royal palace, all the houses, and all the public buildings in Jerusalem. Then the entire army surrounded the city walls and tore them down, stone by stone.

"He carried into exile to Babylon the remnant, who escaped from the sword, and they became servants to him and his sons until the

---

[50] Jeremiah 21:3-7.
[51] 2 Kings 25:7.
[52] 2 Chronicles 36:17.

kingdom of Persia came to power."[53]

Shortly after their arrival, the exiles received a letter from God, care of the prophet Jeremiah and delivered by two men named Elasah and Gemariah. The text of that letter has survived to this day.

It began with greetings from "the Lord Almighty, the God of Israel" to "all those I carried into exile from Jerusalem to Babylon." In it, the Lord instructed the exiles to "build houses and settle down; plant gardens and eat what they produce. Marry and have sons and daughters; find wives for your sons and give your daughters in marriage, so that they too may have sons and daughters. Increase in number there; do not decrease. Also, seek the peace and prosperity of the city to which I have carried you into exile. Pray to the Lord for it, because if it prospers, you too will prosper. Do not let the prophets and diviners among you deceive you. Do not listen to the dreams you encourage them to have. They are prophesying lies to you in my name. I have not sent them."

The Lord went on to assure them that they will not remain in captivity forever. He assured them that he was not finished with them.

> When seventy years are completed for Babylon, I will come to you and fulfill my gracious promise to bring you back to this place. For I know the plans I have for you, plans to prosper you and not to harm you,

[53] 2 Chronicles 36:20.

> plans to give you hope and a future. Then you will call upon me and come and pray to me, and I will listen to you. You will seek me and find me when you seek me with all your heart. I will be found by you and will bring you back from captivity."[54]

The letter also rebuked some of the exiles by name, signed the death warrants of the false prophets among them, installed new priests, and reminded them that the reason they were sent into exile was the hope that they would repent.

Once again, we witness God's fathomless mercy and compassion for his people. But we also see his love for Iraq.

Centuries later, a man named Paul would write that God's intent is that, "through the church, the manifold wisdom of God should be made known to the rulers and authorities in the heavenly realms, according to his eternal purpose which he accomplished in Christ Jesus our Lord."[55]

In the same way, God's intent for the rulers and authorities in Babylon was that his manifold wisdom should be made known to them through the church, that is, through the faithful remnant among the exiles.

God's desire and man's choices, however, do not always agree.

---

[54] Jeremiah 29:4-14.

[55] Ephesians 3:10-11.

God wanted Israel to obey its covenant with him. But even as he transferred the responsibility for his people from Moses to Joshua, the Lord admitted that “these people will soon prostitute themselves to the foreign gods of the land they are entering. They will forsake me and break the covenant I made with them.”[56]

Peter reveals that God is patient with us, “not wanting anyone to perish.”[57] But Jesus concedes that, “wide is the gate and broad is the road that leads to destruction, and many enter through it. But small is the gate and narrow the road that leads to life, and only a few find it.”[58]

And despite the best efforts of the “missionaries” he sent to Babylon, the empire would fail.

When Judah’s seventy years of captivity ended, God warned, “I will punish the king of Babylon and his nation, the land of the Babylonians, for their guilt, and will make it desolate forever.... They themselves will be enslaved by many nations and great kings; I will repay them according to their deeds and the work of their hands.”[59]

Had they repented, as Nineveh did, albeit briefly, perhaps God may yet have relented and with compassion turned from his fierce anger, so that they would not have perished.

---

[56] Deuteronomy 31:16.
[57] 2 Peter 3:9.
[58] Matthew 7:13-14.
[59] Jeremiah 25:11, 14.

The seven most prominent exiles in Babylon were Ezekiel, Daniel, Ezra and Nehemiah, Hananiah, Mishael, and Azariah (whose names were changed by the prince of the eunuchs to Shadrach, Meshack, and Abednego and whose story was popularized in the 1930s and 1940s by Louis Armstrong, The Golden Gate Quartette, Benny Goodman, and others).

Ezekiel was among the first to go into captivity, along with king Jehoiachin, in 597 B.C., eleven years before the fall of Jerusalem. When he arrived, he did exactly as the Lord commanded. He built a house in the midst of a community of exiles in Tel-abib, along the River Chebar, a canal southeast of Babylon.

He was a priest, the son of a priest. And, as both priest and prophet, he was esteemed by the Jewish elders who frequently consulted him concerning the future of Jerusalem and the exiles. We also know that Ezekiel was married, but his wife seems to have died suddenly and unexpectedly, some think of a stroke.

> In the thirty-seventh year of the exile of Jehoiachin king of Judah, in the year Evil-Merodach became king of Babylon, he released Jehoiachin from prison on the twenty-seventh day of the twelfth
>
> month. He spoke kindly to him and gave him a seat of honor higher than those of the other kings who were with him in Babylon. So Jehoiachin put aside his prison clothes and for

> the rest of his life ate regularly at the king's table. Day by day the king gave Jehoiachin a regular allowance as long as he lived.[60]

So what happened to Ezekiel? Did he ever leave Babylon? Did he ever return to Israel?

According to tradition, the prophet is buried in central Iraq, in a small village called Kifl.

Yigal Schleifer, a freelance journalist based in Istanbul, wrote of his first visit to the site:

> Kifl itself is a dusty, forlorn-feeling town of one-story mud-brick homes. Finding the site of Ezekiel's grave was surprisingly easy—the ziggurat-like, mud-colored top of the shrine built around it was visible as soon as we entered the town.
>
> Soon somebody came to tell us the shrine was open and as we approached it, we stepped around the gray-colored sewage that was running down the middle of the narrow alleyways.
>
> According to former Baghdady Jews, large numbers of them would make a pilgrimage to the shrine for the holiday of Shavuot, sleeping in the small rooms of the building that encloses the peaceful courtyard,

[60] 2 Kings 25:27.

where olive, palm and fig trees grow.

Little is known about the death of Ezekiel, but his tomb is mentioned by the 12th century Jewish traveler Benjamin of Tudela, who describes it as revered by both Jews and Muslims, though in the care of Jews, with a large library of Jewish books inside, including some dating from the time of the First Temple.

We took off our shoes and entered the shrine through a green wooden door into what was clearly once a synagogue, with Hebrew writing running across one wall. Under one arched doorway, a Hebrew inscription reads: “And this gravestone is the gravestone of our prophet Ezekiel.” Two elderly Muslim men were in one corner, prostrating themselves in prayer. In another room also filled with Hebrew inscriptions, under a spectacular roof created out of right angles, sits a large wood-paneled

vault. The walls, which are painted with a floral design that is faded but still exquisite, also have glass inlaid in them, giving the room a jewel-like quality. The caretaker, a 50-year-old named Abu Khadum,

> opened a small door near the front of the crypt and told me to look inside. The wood was covering a much older stone tomb that had two tablets engraved with Hebrew at the front. I couldn't make out the writing on them except for one word, which was the name *Yehezhel.*[61]

While Ezekiel's ministry was exclusively to comfort the exiles, Daniel's was to convict the king. Ezekiel was about twenty-five years old when he was taken into captivity. Daniel, along with his three companions—Hananiah, Mishael, and Azariah—were still youths. Ezekiel was a priest; Daniel was an aristocrat. Ezekiel's exile was spent in a small village; Daniel lived in the royal palaces of Nebuchadnezzar and Belshazzar, Babylon's last kings, as well as in the palaces of the Median king, Darius, and King Cyrus of Persia.

The Book of Daniel opens with a fascinating peek into palace life and the character and personality of one of Iraq's greatest rulers.

In addition to his awesome military conquests, Nebuchadnezzar was a man who thirsted after knowledge and beauty. He was zealous for his gods, invested tremendous sums in the structure and maintenance of their temples, and surrounded himself with

---

[61] Yigal Schleifer, "Iraq: Where Judaism Began." Reprinted by permission.

magicians, enchanters, sorcerers, and astrologers.

He was extravagant not only to his gods but also to those who had his favor. For example, tradition holds that he built the legendary hanging gardens for his homesick Median wife, Amyitis. And after Daniel interpreted the king's dream, he elevated all four young men to positions of great power and influence, presenting them with rich gifts.

اسأل الهجن

Ask Gamali!

What made the hanging gardens a wonder of the world?

After a visit, Historian Diodorus Siculus said that "The approach to the Garden sloped like a hillside and the several parts of the structure rose from one another tier on tier . . . On all this, the earth had been piled . . . and was thickly planted with trees of every kind that, by their great size and other charm, gave pleasure to the beholder . . . The water machines [raised] the water in great abundance from the river, although no one outside could see it." He went on to explain that the platforms on which the garden stood consisted of huge slabs of stone, [unusual, since everything else in Babylon was of brick] covered with layers of reed, asphalt and tiles. Over this was put "a covering with sheets of lead, that the wet which drenched through the earth might not rot the foundation. Upon all these was laid earth of a convenient depth, sufficient for the growth of the greatest trees. When the soil was laid even and smooth, it was planted with all sorts of trees, which both for greatness and beauty might delight the spectators." The expanse of the gardens, according to Diodorus, was about 400 feet square and more than 80 feet high. Other estimates put the gardens as high as the outer city walls, about 320 feet.

Despite his generosity, however, the king had two great faults that would prove his downfall. First, he thought too highly of himself. Second, he thought to little of God.

Nebuchadnezzar basked in the glory of all his magnificent accomplishments, once declaring as he walked along the palace roof, "Is not this the great Babylon I have built as the royal residence, by my mighty power and for the glory of my majesty?"[62]

No sooner had the words passed his lips than the voice of the Lord thundered from heaven:

> "Your royal authority has been taken from you. You will be driven away from people and will live with the wild animals; you will eat grass like cattle. Seven times will pass by for you until you acknowledge that the Most High is sovereign over the kingdoms of men and gives them to anyone he wishes."[63]

Scripture confirms that this amazing prophecy was fulfilled immediately.

> He was driven away from his people and ate grass like cattle. His body was drenched with the dew of heaven until his hair grew like the feathers of an eagle and his nails like the claws of a bird.

In his own recorded testimony, the chastened monarch says, "At the end of that time, I, Nebuchadnezzar, raised my eyes toward heaven, and my sanity was restored. Then I praised the Most High; I honored and glorified him who lives forever. His dominion is an eternal dominion; his kingdom endures from

---

[62] Daniel 4:29.
[63] Daniel 4:30-32.

generation to generation. All the peoples of the earth are regarded as nothing. He does as he pleases with the powers of heaven and the peoples of the earth. No one can hold back his hand or say to him, 'What have you done?'"

Then his kingdom was restored, even greater than before. And the king declared, "Now I, Nebuchadnezzar, praise and exalt and glorify the King of heaven, because everything he does is right and all his ways are just. And those who walk in pride he is able to humble."[64]

But Belshazzar, his successor, failed to learn this lesson. And in the middle of "a great banquet for a thousand of his nobles," the new king saw something that turned his face pale and buckled his knees.

A human finger appeared in midair and wrote four words on the wall: "Mene, Mene, Tekel, Parsin," which Daniel interpreted for him as, "God has numbered the days of your reign and brought it to an end. You have been weighed on the scales and found wanting. Your kingdom is divided and given to the Medes and Persians."

That same night, Belshazzar was murdered, "and Darius the Mede took over the kingdom, at the age of sixty-two."[65]

The ruthless conquest of Babylon by Persia (modern Iran) in 539 B.C. was graphically described by Isaiah:

> Wail, for the day of the Lord is near;
> it will come like destruction from

---

[64] Daniel 4:33-37.
[65] Daniel 5:30.

the Almighty. Because of this, all hands will go limp, every man's heart will melt. Terror will seize them, pain and anguish will grip them; they will writhe like a woman in labor. They will look aghast at each other, their faces aflame. See, the day of the Lord is coming—a cruel day, with wrath and fierce anger … Whoever is captured will be thrust through; all who are caught will fall by the sword. Their infants will be dashed to pieces before their eyes; their houses will be looted and their wives ravished. See, I will stir up against them the Medes [of Media in northwestern Iran], who do not care for silver and have no delight in gold. Their bows will strike down the young men; they will have no mercy on infants nor will they look with compassion on

children. Babylon, the jewel of kingdoms, the glory of the Babylonians' pride, will be overthrown by God like Sodom and Gomorrah. She will never be inhabited or lived in through all generations; no Arab will pitch his tent there, no shepherd will rest his flocks there."[66]

---

[66] Isaiah 13:6-9, 15-20.

Again, Isaiah prophesied:

> Like whirlwinds sweeping through the southland, an invader comes from the desert, from a land of terror. A dire vision has been shown to me: The traitor betrays, the looter takes loot. Elam [southwestern Iran], attack! Media, lay siege! I will bring to an end all the groaning she caused.… And the lookout shouted, "Day after day, my lord, I stand on the watchtower, every night I stay at my post. Look, here comes a man in a chariot with a team of horses. And he gives back the answer: 'Babylon has fallen, has fallen! All the images of its gods like shattered on the ground!'"[67]

And again:

> Sit in silence, go into darkness, Daughter of the Babylonians; no more will you be called queen of kingdoms. I was angry with my people and desecrated my inheritance; I gave them into your hand, and you showed them no mercy. Even on the aged you laid a very heavy yoke. You said, "I will continue forever—the eternal queen!" … Now then, listen, you

[67] Isaiah 21:1-2, 8-9.

> wanton creature, lounging in your security and saying to yourself, "I am, and there is none besides me. I will never be a widow or suffer the loss of children." Both of these will overtake you in a moment, on a single day."[68]

Yet, again:

> Listen to me, O Jacob, Israel, whom I have called: I am he; I am the first and I am the last.... Come together, all of you, and listen: Which of the idols has foretold these things? The Lord's chosen ally will carry out his purpose against Babylon; his arm will be against the Babylonians. I, even I, have spoken; yes, I have called him. I will bring him, and he will succeed in his mission."[69]

Persia succeeded too well in its terrible and ruthless mission. And to this day, Babylon remains a desolate, uninhabited ruin.

Darius was succeeded by Cyrus, who released the exiles to return to Jerusalem. Daniel, however, never returned. And we have only rumors and traditions concerning his final years and death.

> During the Middle Ages, there was a widespread and persistent tradition

---

[68] Isaiah 47:5-7, 8-9.
[69] Isaiah 48:12, 14-15.

that Daniel was buried at Susa, the modern Shuster, in the Persian province of Khuzistan. In the account of his visit to Susa in A.D. 1165, Rabbi Benjamin of Tudela narrates that Daniel's tomb was shown him in the façade of one of

the synagogues of that city; and it is shown there to the present day. The Roman martyrology assigns Daniel's feast as a holy prophet to 21 July, and apparently treats Babylon as his burial-place.[70]

اسأل الهجن

ASK GAMALI!

What is Babylon like today?

In 1983, Saddam Hussein started rebuilding the city on top of the old ruins, investing in both restoration and new construction. He inscribed his name on many of the bricks in imitation of Nebuchadnezzar. One frequent inscription reads: "This was built by Saddam Hussein, son of Nebuchadnezzar, to glorify Iraq." These bricks became sought after as collectors' items after the downfall of Hussein, and the ruins are no longer being restored to their original state. He also installed a huge portrait of himself and Nebuchadnezzar at the entrance to the ruins, and shored up Processional Way, a large boulevard of ancient stones, and the Lion of Babylon, a black rock sculpture about 2,600 years old. When the First Gulf War ended, Saddam wanted to build a modern palace, also over some old ruins; it was made in the pyramidal style of a Sumerian ziggurat. He named it Saddam Hill. In 2003, he was ready to begin the construction of a cable car line over Babylon when the invasion began and halted the project.

http://en.wikipedia.org/wiki/Babylon#Reconstruction

Like Ezekiel, Ezra was a priest and an exile in Babylon. He is credited with writing the books of Ezra and Nehemiah (which in the original Hebrew Scriptures were actually one

[70] The Catholic Encyclopedia, 1913 .

book) and is traditionally believed to be the author of the Chronicles.

The Book of Ezra begins in 539 B.C. when Cyrus released the Jewish captives and allowed them to leave Iraq to rebuild Jerusalem under the leadership of Zerubbabel.

In 458 B.C., after much opposition against the vanguard, Ezra returned to Jerusalem with a second group of exiles. In Ezra's account, this group consisted of 42,360 exiles, in addition to 7,337 servants, 200 singers, 736 horses, 245 mules, 435 camels, and 6,720 donkeys."[71]

The book includes the text of correspondence between the exiles and the Iraqi rulers and continues through Nehemiah, who served in exile as cupbearer to Artaxerxes, the Persian king, and as governor of Jerusalem following his return.

---

[71] Ezra 2:64-67.

Chapter Seven

Iraq appears in one other surprising place in the Old Testament, this time in connection with a popular community leader named Job, who lived in the land of Uz, not to be confused with Oz, which is another story altogether.

The actual location of Uz is unknown. Theories include northwestern Saudi Arabia, western Jordan, or southern Syria. We do, however, know something about Job's enemies.

"The Chaldeans (from southern Iraq) formed three raiding parties and swept down on your camels and carried them off. They put the servants to the sword …"[72]

And we know about Job's three famous friends, particularly the man named Bildad.

Bildad was a Shuhite, a term used exclusively in the Bible to describe Bildad and which appears only in the Book of Job. Historians tell us that the Shuhites were among the Bene-Kedem, "a people dwelling to the east of Jordan, by which we are to understand not so much the Arabian desert, that reaches to the Euphrates, as Mesopotamia."[73]

This being so, Bildad would have been an Iraqi.

Bildad spoke three times to Job, but his theology impressed neither Job nor God. For, when all was said and done, the Lord rebuked Bildad and his chums.

---

[72] Job 1:17.

[73] Idem, Merrill F. Unger, p. 134.

“I am angry with you,” he said, “because you have not spoken of me what is right, as my servant Job has.” And the Lord commanded Bildad and his friends to “take seven bulls and seven rams and go to my servant Job and sacrifice a burnt offering for yourselves. My servant Job will pray for you, and I will accept his prayer and not deal with you according to your folly.”[74]

---

[74] Job 42:7-8.

Chapter Eight

Moving into the New Testament, we find the next mention of Iraq in Matthew's Gospel. The genealogy of Jesus in the first chapter utilizes Iraq as a generational marker.

> … and Josiah the father of Jeconiah and his brothers at the time of the exile to Babylon. After the exile to Babylon: Jeconiah was the father of Shealtiel, Shealtiel the father of Zerubbabel …[75]

> Thus there were fourteen generations in all from Abraham to David, fourteen from David to the exile to Babylon, and fourteen from the exile to the Christ.[76]

Jesus' disciples were gathered together in a private room in Jerusalem, following his ascension into heaven.

> Suddenly a sound like the blowing of a violent wind came from heaven and filled the whole house where they were sitting. They saw what seemed to be tongues of fire that separated and came to rest on each of them. All of them were filled with the Holy Spirit and began to

---

[75] Matthew 1:11-12.

[76] Matthew 1:17.

> speak in other tongues as the Spirit enabled them.
>
> Now there were staying in Jerusalem God-fearing Jews from every nation under heaven. When they heard this sound, a crowd came together in bewilderment, because each one heard them speaking in his own language. Utterly amazed, they asked: "Are not all these men who are speaking Galileans? Then how is it that each of us hears them in his own native language? Parthians, Medes and Elamites; residents of Mesopotamia, Judea and Cappadocia, Pontus and Asia, Phrygia and Pamphylia, Egypt and the parts of Libya near Cyrene; visitors from Rome (both Jews and converts to Judaism); Cretans and Arabs—we hear them declaring the wonders of God in our own tongues!" Amazed and perplexed, they asked one another, "What does this mean?"[77]

Elamites and residents of Mesopotamia were Iraqi Jews. There at Pentecost. Listening to Peter share the Good News of Jesus Christ. And "Those who accepted his message were baptized, and about three thousand were added to their number that day."[78]

---

[77] Acts 2:2-12.
[78] Acts 2:41.

And if these Iraqi Jews were among those newly-baptized believers, they surely returned to their homes in Elam and Mesopotamia, carrying with them the presence and Gospel of Jesus Christ.

Later in Acts, we are introduced to a young man named Stephen, "a man full of God's grace and power," who briefly refers to Iraq after his arrest by the Sanhedrin.

Quoting the prophet Amos, he says, "'You have lifted up the shrine of Molech and the star of your god Rephan, the idols you made to worship. Therefore I will send you into exile' beyond Babylon."[79]

At the close of his letter to the Christians in Asia Minor, Peter wrote, "She who is in Babylon, chosen together with you, sends you her greetings, and so does my son Mark."[80]

There are several theories of who "she" might be.

"Some think it to have been a greeting from Peter's wife, a noble person who accompanied Peter on his journeys and who, tradition says, was martyred before her husband. She would have been well known to Peter's readers."[81]

The *Amplified Bible*, *Good News Bible*, and *International Standard Version* translate the passage as "your sister church" in Babylon.

Either way, the reference alludes to Iraq.

---

[79] Acts 7:43.

[80] 1 Peter 5:13.

[81] Everett F. Harrison, *The Wycliffe Bible Commentary* (Moody Press, Chicago) 1962, p. 1452.

Babylon is mentioned half a dozen times in the last book of the Bible. This time, however, it is allegorical and does not speak directly to the physical city in southern Iraq.

There are many suppositions concerning Babylon's politico/eschatological identity, But the key seems to be in the first five words of the book: "The revelation of Jesus Christ."

Babylon represents everything antithetical to Jesus—whether social, philosophical, or theological, scientific or political.

We have a final glimpse of Babylon in Revelation 18:21:

> Then a mighty angel picked up a boulder the size of a large millstone and threw it into the sea and said, "With such violence the great city of Babylon will be thrown down, never to be found again. The music of harpists and musicians, flute players and trumpeters, will never be heard in you again. No workman of any trade will ever be heard in you again. The sound of a millstone will never be heard in you again. The light of a lamp will never shine in you again. The voice of bridegroom and bride will never be heard in you
>
> again. Your merchants were the world's great men. By your magic spell all the nations were led astray. In her was found the blood of

> prophets and of the saints, and of all
> who have been killed on the earth."

But the fate of Babylon is not the future of Iraq. Iraq is not Babylon. Iraq is God's "handiwork." And it is not destroyed, never to rise again. Iraq is alive and destined to be "a blessing on the earth."

Now that we have traced Iraq in God's Word, we'll look at the effects of God's Word in Iraq.

Chapter Nine

As Mesopotamia was the Cradle of Civilization, the region between the Caspian Sea and the Mediterranean was the Cradle of Christianity. And representatives of most of the early Christian churches still live in those countries today.

Several traditions account for the arrival of the gospel in Iraq.

One says it was the new Iraqi believers, who had accepted Christ at Pentecost, who evangelized their people. Another credits the apostle Thomas who they say preached the gospel in Mesopotamia en route to India. A third says Iraq was evangelized after Stephen, one of the seven deacons, was stoned to death.

> On that day a great persecution broke out against the church at Jerusalem, and all except the apostles were scattered throughout Judea and Samaria.[82]

Luke continues his account to his friend, Theophilus, by detailing the journeys of Philip, Paul, Peter, Barnabas and Mark.

> Then Barnabas went to Tarsus to look for Saul, and when he found him, he brought him to Antioch. So for a whole year Barnabas and Saul

---

[82] Acts 8:1.

> met with the church and taught great numbers of people.[83]

And here in Antioch, in southern Turkey, the disciples were first referred to as "Christians."

Throughout the first few centuries, the church was troubled by several critical theological disputes.

The first, which Luke recorded in Acts 15:29, was over circumcision and the Levitical laws.

Some Christ-followers held that Gentile believers should be required to be circumcised and to obey the laws of Moses. Paul and Silas disagreed violently, prompting the first ecumenical council at Jerusalem. The council's decision was dispatched via Paul and Barnabas and two prophets named Judas and Silas to the Gentiles in Antioch, Syria, and Cilicea. It said that Gentiles need only "abstain from food sacrificed to idols, from blood, from the meat of strangled animals and from sexual immorality." Nothing more, as far as law was concerned.

Over the next few centuries, more explosive disputes arose.

In 306, Constantine I (Flavius Valerius Aurelius Constantinus) ascended the Roman throne. Six years later, he defeated his rival, Maxentius, at the amazing Battle of Milvian Bridge.

Legend says that, just before the battle, the forty-year-old emperor saw a vision of a cross.

---

[83] Acts 11:25-26.

Written on it were the words: "By this sign thou shalt conquer."

From then on, the cross was emblazoned on every shield and banner and Christians were shown favoritism throughout the empire.

The Church grew very large and prosperous. But as it expanded, heresies seeped in, the most divisive being over the definition of the Trinity.

What was the relationship between the Father and Jesus? Who was the Holy Ghost? Was Jesus God? Was he human? Did he have one nature or two, one person or two?

The church was threatened with schism.

So in 325, Constantine called a council of churchmen to meet in Nicaea (today, a popular resort city at the foot of the Alps on the French Riviera near the Italian border). The result of the council was what is known today as *The Nicene Creed*:

> We believe in one God, the Father Almighty, maker of all things, both visible and invisible; and in one Lord, Jesus Christ, the Son of God, Only begotten of the Father, that is to say, of the substance of the Father, God of God and Light of Light, very God of very God, begotten, not made, being of one substance with the Father, by whom all things were made, both things in heaven and things on earth; who, for us men and for our salvation, came

> down and was made flesh, was made man, suffered, and rose again on the third day, went up into the heavens, and is to come again to judge both the quick and the dead; and in the Holy Ghost.

Most Christians embraced this decree. Nevertheless, debate continued over the nature of Christ, as well as how, if he was God, he could be born of a woman.

Nestorius, a monk in the monastery of Euprepius, entered the debate after being appointed Patriarch in Constantinople in 428. He stirred up a hornets nest by declaring that, while Jesus indeed possesses two *natures*, he is also two separate and distinct *persons*—one human and one divine. Three years later, he was renounced at the Council at Ephesus, condemned as a heretic, and exiled.

The second Council at Ephesus in 449 approved another theory called *monophysitism,* which stated that God entered completely into Jesus through a kind of incarnation. It was God who was born, died, and rose from the dead through Jesus, thereby making Mary the mother of God.

Two years later, another council was called, in Chalcedon in Asia Minor. It concluded:

> Therefore, following the holy fathers, we all with one accord teach men to acknowledge one and the same Son, our Lord Jesus Christ, at

once complete in Godhead and complete in manhood, truly God and truly man, consisting also of a reasonable soul and body; of one substance with the Father as regards his Godhead, and at the same time of one substance with us as regards his manhood; like us in all respects, apart from sin; as regards his Godhead, begotten of the Father before the ages, but yet as regards his manhood begotten, for us men and for our salvation, of Mary the Virgin, the God-bearer; one and the same Christ, Son, Lord, Only-begotten, recognized in two natures, without confusion, without change, without division, without separation; the distinction of natures being in no way annulled by the union, but rather the characteristics of each nature being preserved and coming together to form one person and subsistence, not as parted or separated into two persons, but one and the same Son and Only-begotten God the Word, Lord Jesus Christ; even as the prophets from earliest times spoke of him, and our Lord Jesus Christ himself taught us, and the creed of the fathers has handed down to us.

Most churches agreed with the councils of Nicaea, Constantinople, and Ephesus. But they were divided over Chalcedon.

On the yea side were the Byzantine, Roman Catholic, Greek Orthodox, and most Protestant Churches (though the Protestant Churches were not present at the meeting). The major churches on the nay side were the Coptic, Syrian Orthodox, and Armenian Orthodox churches, as well as the Nestorians, today known more commonly as the Church of the East.

The Church of the East

The Church of the East traces its roots to the second century Church in Edessa (modern Urfa in southeast Turkey) and its doctrine to Nestorius.

When Mongol general Tamerlane conquered Persia (Iran), Mesopotamia (Iraq), and Syria at the end of the fourteenth century, he destroyed nearly all of the civilian population, including most Nestorians.

In 1551, the Nestorian Church split into two movements, each bearing the names of the people who lived in the regions. The Assyrians maintained their Nestorian heritage, while the Chaldeans aligned themselves with the Catholic Church in Rome.

Then, on November 11, 1994, Pope John Paul II and Mar Dinkha IV, Patriarch of the Assyrian Church of the East, signed a "Common Christological Declaration" of faith and beliefs.

In this document the Assyrian Church of the East agreed that Jesus Christ "is not an 'ordinary man' whom God adopted in order to reside in him and inspire him, as in the righteous ones and the prophets. But the same God the Word, begotten of his Father before all worlds without beginning according to his divinity, was born of a mother without a father in the last times according to his humanity." Jesus "is true God and true man, perfect in his divinity and perfect in his humanity, consubstantial with the Father and consubstantial with us in all things but sin. His divinity and his humanity are united in one person, without confusion or change, without division or separation….the divinity and humanity are united in the person of the same and unique Son of God and Lord."[84]

The Armenian Apostolic Church

In Iraq, the Armenian Apostolic Church, also called the Armenian Orthodox Church, is centralized mostly in Baghdad. Its tradition holds that Armenia was evangelized by the apostles Bartholomew and Thaddeus.

The founder of the Armenian Orthodox Church was Gregor Lusarovitch, known as Saint Gregory the Illuminator.

Lusarovitch was born in 257 A.D. in Cappadocia and dedicated his life to bringing Christianity to Armenia. Unfortunately, he was the son of the enemy of Armenian King

[84] Special thanks to Dan Lundberg in Stockholm whose article: "Christians from the Middle East" (http://www.visarkiv.se/mmm/media/assyrien/religi-e.htm) helped to provide a clear outline for this portion of a rather complex history.

Tiridates I, which was enough to get him thrown into prison for fourteen years. Eventually, the king went mad, and Lusarovitch was brought out of prison to intercede with God for him. The king was healed and, as a result, Armenia in 301 A.D. became the first nation in the world to make Christianity its state religion.

Two centuries later, it was caught up in a war with the Persians who were trying to force the Armenian nation to return to Zoroastrianism (a religion that began in Persia that worships the god Ormazd—creator of the world, source of light, and embodiment of good). Because of this, the Armenian Apostolic Church was unable to send representatives to the Council of Chalcedon. After the Council's declaration was published, the Armenian Apostolic Church, along with the Syrian Orthodox and Copts, parted from the Catholic/Orthodox churches.

Then, in the seventh century, a group split off from the Armenian Apostolic Church and allied itself with Rome as the Armenian Catholic Church. Nevertheless, its identity remained distinctly Armenian, and its liturgy is in the classic Armenian language.

The Syrian Orthodox Church

Tradition holds that the Syrian Church—also known as the Jacobites, after the sixth century bishop, Jacob Baradaeus—was established by the apostle Peter in 37 A.D. Syrian Christians speak Syriac, a language close to Aramaic.

As an expression of their belief that Christ has only a divine nature, they make the sign of the cross with a single finger.

In the seventeenth century, the church split, as some members submitted themselves to the Roman Pope and became the Syrian Catholic Church.

The Kurdish Church

An estimated twenty-two million ethnic Kurds live in a mountainous territory roughly the size of Nebraska. Most are Sunni Muslim and speak a variety of dialects of a unique Kurdish language akin to Farsi.

One of the most famous Kurds was the twelfth century Muslim warrior Saladin, who unified the Muslim world and recaptured Jerusalem from the Crusaders.

After World War I, the Kurds were promised their own state, carved out of the former Ottoman Empire. Then oil was discovered, and Kurdistan was absorbed by Turkey, Iran, Iraq, and Syria.

Since the 1920s, hostilities have continued between Iraq's Kurds and Baghdad over Kurdish independence. In addition to self-government and maintaining their own militia, the Iraqi Kurds want what they see as their share in national oil revenues.

These hostilities reached a new low in 1988 when Saddam Hussein launched an operation known as “al-Anfal” designed to ruthlessly exterminate the entire Iraqi Kurdish population.

> The attacks resulted in the death of at least fifty thousand (some reports estimate as many as one hundred thousand people), many of them women and children. A team of Human Rights Watch investigators determined, after analyzing eighteen tons of captured Iraqi documents, testing soil samples and carrying out interviews with more than three hundred fifty witnesses, that the attacks on the Kurdish people were characterized by gross violations of human rights, including mass executions and disappearances of many tens of thousands of noncombatants; widespread use of chemical weapons including Sarin, mustard gas, and nerve agents that killed thousands; the arbitrary imprisoning of tens of thousands of women, children, and elderly people for months in conditions of extreme deprivation; forced displacement of hundreds of thousands of villagers after the demolition of their homes; and the wholesale destruction of nearly two thousand villages, along with their schools, mosques, farms, and power stations.[85]

After the first Gulf War in 1991, the Holy Spirit began to move in power among the

[85] http://en.wikipedia.org/wiki/Human_rights_violations_in_Iraq.

Kurdish people in northern Iraq, until today about three hundred born-again Christians live in the midst of three-and-a-half million Kurds.

According to one missionary working among the Kurds, these believers have "a vision for reaching out and planting other churches in Kurdistan, despite seemingly overwhelming opposition. The verse that God has given the church leadership is 'Ask of me and I will make the nations your inheritance.'"[86]

While the Kurdish-speaking church in Iraq is open to all, its mission is to reach its own people. To accomplish this, it respects and protects Kurdish language, culture, and heritage.

"It is a small church," the missionary adds, "often struggling, but eager to live out the love which they have found in Christ."

Iraqi Muslims

Islam's largest groups are the Sunni (90 percent of all Muslims) and the Shi'a (which split away from the Sunni in 661).

While many additional differences developed over the years, the chief dispute between the two groups continues to be over who is the rightful leader of Islam.

Historian Jonathan Frazier explains:

> When Mohammad died, he left no successor. The Sunnis said it should be the one who is most able. The Shi'a said, no, it should be the one who is the physical or spiritual heir.

[86] Psalm 2:8.

> Mohammad had no sons, but he did have daughters. And Fatima, one of the daughters, married a man named Ali, who had a son, who would be Mohammad's grandson. So the Shi'a follow the descendants; the Sunni elect the most able.

In an effort to drive coalition forces out of Iraq, terrorists are reportedly stirring up ancient conflicts between the Sunni and Shi'a.

According to *The York Times,* U.S. officials intercepted an undated seventeen-page letter written by Abu Musab al-Zarqawi—a Jordanian with suspected ties to Al Qaeda—to senior leaders of the terrorist organization.

"Mounting an attack on Iraq's Shiite majority could rescue the movement," the article said. The document contends that the aim of such attacks is to prompt a counterattack against the Arab Sunni minority.

This, wrote al-Zarqawi, "is the only way to prolong the duration of the fight between the infidels and us. If we succeed in dragging them into a sectarian war, this will awaken the sleepy Sunnis who are fearful of destruction and death at the hands" of Shiites.

The *Times* article says the document warned that the attacks had to be under way before the turnover of sovereignty in June. If not, "any attacks on Shiites will be viewed as Iraqi-on-Iraqi violence that will find little support among the people."

Al-Zarqawi is also quoted as taking responsibility for scores of suicide bombings inside Iraq.

"We were involved in all the martyrdom operations—in terms of overseeing, preparing and planning—that took place in this country. Praise be to Allah, I have completed twenty-five of these operations, some of them against the Shi'a and their leaders, the Americans and their military, and the police, the military, and the coalition forces."[87]

The Church Today

In the early years of the 20th century, seventy percent of the Christian population was concentrated in the north. But conflicts with the Kurds, the war with Iran (three times larger than Iraq), and the repeated and relentless bombing of their villages by Saddam—as well as worsening economic hardships—drove many to Baghdad and caused many more to emigrate.

Since 1991, an estimated one-third of Iraqi Christians have fled the country.

As with historical churches throughout the world, including in the West, not all of the five percent of the Iraqi population that identifies itself as Christian are born-again followers of Christ. Estimates vary, however, as to the actual size of the remnant.

---

87 Dexter Filkins, "U.S. Says Files Seek Al Qaeda Aid in Iraq Conflict," *The New York Times*, February 8, 2004 (http://aolsvc.news.aol.com/news/article.adp?id=20040209990011).

Under Saddam, the Assyrian Presbyterian Church and the Arab Presbyterian Church were the only two recognized evangelical churches in Baghdad. Over time, the Arab Presbyterian Church became more evangelistic, and many "nominal Christians" from the historical churches were drawn to it. Today, these believers are the majority in the church.

Shortly after the capture of Saddam Hussein, many new evangelical churches—including Independent Baptist, Southern Baptist, Alliance, Methodist, United Pentecostal, and Assemblies of God—were established throughout the country, as refugees who had fled the two Gulf wars returned to Iraq. Among them were many who had accepted Christ in other countries, as well as some who had attended seminaries in Jordan or Lebanon and were now eager to establish churches without government interference or fear of arrest.

The strength of the remnant lies in its faith, not in its numbers—faith that has been tested and purified in the crucible of Saddam Hussein's bloody regime.

Iraqi Christians are no longer in danger from tyranny. Today, their greatest threat lies in being caught in the crossfire, as Sunni and Shiite Muslims fight for control of the new government.

But it takes much more than a historical primer to begin to understand the Church in Iraq. It requires us to visit with some of our brothers and sisters, to hear their hearts and share their spirits.

Chapter Ten

Reverend Ghassam Thomas is president of the Christian & Missionary Alliance (C&MA) Church in Iraq and pastor of the Alliance Church in Baghdad. He is married, and he and his wife have two children.

Growing up in Saddam's Iraq, Ghassam Thomas was discontent.

"I wanted to marry, to have nice things. I wanted to leave my country and live in America like my parents. My brother and sister live in Australia. They are not believers, so they searched for real peace in other countries and cultures."

But while Ghassam dreamed of the wonders that he believed awaited him in foreign lands, his cousin was on her knees asking God to show him a different solution.

"She told me about Jesus Christ and prayed for me for ten years. In 1992, I went to the Evangelical Presbyterian Church in Baghdad to buy a Bible, where I heard some preaching and Christian songs. Someone came up to me and spoke to me about Jesus Christ, and I was born again. I promised God then that I would be a pastor."

Four years later, Ghassam went to Lebanon to study theology.

"I studied from 1996 to 1999. Then I returned to Iraq and tried to start an Alliance church. But there was much opposition from the government. Nevertheless, I wanted to be here, so I got the idea to open a kindergarten. At the same time, I led underground services in my home and in the homes of others. Also, friends in Jordan and Lebanon gave me money to buy food to distribute to poor people.

"While there was no direct persecution of Christians in Iraq during Saddam's regime, there was indirect persecution.

"One day, one of Saddam's soldiers, a captain, came to my house and asked me, 'Do you teach theology in your kindergarten?'

"I said no.

"He asked, 'Did you open the kindergarten to speak with the people about the Bible?'

"I said no.

"He said, 'We will have to arrest you if you do that.'

"In other words, the government basically told us, 'We have no problem with Christians, but don't meet in your homes or where you work.'

"One year, I had a New Year's party at my kindergarten, and I preached and we sang Christian songs. The government heard about it and sent soldiers. They asked me why I did that, and I told them that a lot of Muslims did that in their parties. But they warned me not to do that again.

"Finally, one day, a friend called to warn me that the soldiers were coming to arrest me and put me in prison. I believed that they would kill me. I fled from Iraq with my family and went to Jordan. Two days later, my friend called me and told me not to come back because the government was looking for me. Under Saddam, when someone gave food to people in need, the government said he is an American spy.

"So my wife and I prayed. We said, *God, we love Iraq. We want to return. But I cannot return because they will kill me if I return.* We prayed and prayed.

"Three weeks later, the war (Operation Iraqi Freedom) began, and Saddam was done. At that time, five doors were open to us—in Australia, Turkey, Jordan, Lebanon, and Iraq. But our hearts were in Iraq.

"We returned in April, and I began holding services. The people came and, within three weeks, we had no more room. There was no place to sit. They told me, we need a church.

"I saw a good building, but I had no money. I remembered Joshua, when he walked around Jericho. God told him he would give him the land he walked on. Daily, I walked around this building, crying and praying. I told God, *It's not for me; it's for your people.* I cried and I touched the door. *God, I need this building for you.*

"Three days later, a pastor from Lebanon came to me and gave me money.

"'Rent it,' he said. So I rented it.

"Then I prayed, *God, I have this church, but I have no furniture.*

"One day, an elderly Korean man came to a prayer meeting in my home.

"'Are you Pastor Thomas?' he asked me.

"I said yes.

"He said, 'We heard about you in South Korea. We had no money, so we sold chocolates in the road for three weeks, and this is the money for the glory of Jesus.'

"And he gave me $8,000!"

So Pastor Thomas bought all the furniture needed for his church and opened the doors.

Like most people in Iraq today, the families in his congregation are very poor. But their zeal for the Lord more than compensates for their poverty.

"All of our people tithe to the church. They have almost nothing, but they gave like the widow in the Bible. If you give to God, you will be a good believer. There was very little, maybe a total of $50 in a month. But I was very happy about their spirit."

And the Lord multiplied their gifts.

"A church in Lebanon called me and asked if we needed buses.

"I said yes, we need to pick up people and bring them to church, because they are very poor and have no way to get here and there is no public transportation in Baghdad.

"Praise God! They gave me enough money to buy two buses!

"Believe me, God is working, working, working. When you read Mark 12:35-37, it says that there was a large crowd in the temple. Why? Because Jesus was there. Every Sunday, we have four hundred people here—as many as the room will hold. Why? Because Jesus is here. Because the Iraqi people need real peace. People under Saddam were thirsty for righteousness. Now they come to Jesus to quench their thirst.

"Every week, five to ten people—mostly from the historical churches—come to Jesus in this building. They hear the Bible, and they tell me, 'Our eyes have been opened, and we know now who God is.'

"Within the first two months that we were open, I baptized forty-five new believers. And now twenty more are ready. "

Pastor Thomas has a big vision for his country. If you ask him about it, he reaches for his Bible and turns to Isaiah 19:23-25 and reads it to you with passion.

"I always encourage people to stay in Iraq. Don't leave this country. God is going to bless this country and through this country, he will bless the world. It is the last days and Jesus will come quickly."

I asked Pastor Thomas how he felt about Saddam.

"When they showed him on television, I told my church, 'We have a difficult feeling inside. Not happy, not sad. My wife and I pray for him. He is like Nebuchadnezzar. We are praying for a Daniel to go to him. Before I became a Christian, I hated Saddam. After I became a Christian, I didn't love him, but I didn't hate him anymore because Jesus taught me to love everyone."

As for the two Gulf wars, he says, "I believe that God used Saddam Hussein and George Bush and all the leaders in the world. Paul says in Romans 13:1 that "there is no authority except that which God has established." God used them for some work for his glory. Jeremiah 25 speaks of the destruction of Judah by Babylon, yet God called King Nebuchadnezzar 'my servant.'"

BOMBS TARGET IRAQ'S CHRISTIANS, ONE KILLED

Stefan J. Bos, Special Correspondent, ASSIST News Service

BAGHDAD, IRAQ (ANS) Tuesday, January 6, 2004—Iraq's beleaguered Christian minority ushered in the New Year amid grief and fears, after several bombs exploded and at least one believer was killed in a marketplace.

In Basra, about 560 kilometers (350 miles) south of Baghdad, Christians "are grieving the loss of Bashir Toma Elias who was shot in cold blood in the middle of a market place" on Christmas Eve, according to Barnabas Fund, a Christian human rights watchdog.

"Elias was doing last minute Christmas shopping before going home to celebrate with his wife and five children. He was killed with a single shot aimed directly at his head," the organization said.

Journalists covering the story were reportedly told they too would be killed if they continued to talk to "those Christians." Earlier last year, Christian women were attacked and several were killed.

"In Basra in the south, there is a high concentration of Shiite Muslims. They even threaten Christian women to cover their heads," added Saleh Fakhouri, Iraq Coordinator of the Jordan-based Manara Book Ministries, a relief and Christian literature distribution organization (Appendix III). "If she was walking without covering her head, she would be punished in the middle of the street. This is only the beginning."

There are fears among the estimated 100,000 Christians in Basra that Shi'a militia groups, with names like "God's Vengeance," will not rest until all Christians have either left Basra or converted to Islam, Barnabas Fund said. About 2,000 Christian families reportedly have already fled the region.

Pressure is also increasing on a predominantly Christian district of Baghdad after five people died there when a New Years Eve celebration in a restaurant was rocked by a car bomb explosion. "It is not certain that this attack was specifically anti-Christian," said Barnabas Fund, although believers do not rule this out.

But there were apparent miracles in the misery, as Christians "narrowly escaped carnage" when a bomb went off in their church at Christmas.

"The congregation had just celebrated the birth of their Lord with a traditional service when the bomb exploded. Thankfully, no one was hurt, but the blast shattered church windows and caused other damage" a spokesman said.

A week later, as the New Year was ushered in, another bomb was discovered at St. George's monastery in Mosul, about 400 kilometers (250 miles) north of Baghdad. "Again, in the face of potential tragedy, the Christian community had cause to be thankful as it was defused before it could explode."

Chapter Eleven

Joseph Fransees serves as a youth leader in the Alliance Church in Baghdad.

"Pastor Thomas shared the gospel with me and prayed with me, and I kept coming to his home for discipleship and fellowship with other Christians."

Joseph was born in Baghdad in 1977 and grew up in the Armenian Catholic Church.

In high school, he was coerced into joining Saddam's ruling Baath Party.

"The teachers told the students that we would receive between five and ten extra points on our final examination, and that would help us get into university, as well as give us all the privileges accorded to members of the Party. We signed because we didn't know any better, and it seemed like a good thing."

Joseph was admitted to college and, after graduating with an engineering degree, he worked as a nightclub singer (under Saddam, especially as the economy continued to decline under the embargo, even those with college degrees could earn the equivalent of only one or two U.S. dollars a day, so not much of a living could be made as an engineer).

He recalls those years as empty and meaningless.

"I knew nothing about Jesus. My Christianity was limited to Christmas and Easter. But then I heard about this man who gave us salvation, and I knew I could not get rid of all my sins myself. I learned that Jesus' blood could wash me and make me another person."

In 1999, during a youth meeting at Pastor Thomas' house, Joseph gave his life to Christ.

Over the next four years, he grew in faith and his love for the Lord. Then President Bush gave the order that launched Operation Iraqi Freedom.

"I was here in Baghdad, and I was very afraid., especially on the morning when the bombing started and there was fire everywhere. I was praying, and I pictured Jesus walking on the raging sea in the midst of a great storm. And I heard the words, 'Fear not.' It was a word of encouragement that Jesus gave to me. The Lord said, 'The war will be ended in the way that I want this war to be ended, a way that will glorify me. You will not die.' Then, time seemed to stop and I saw a vision of American soldiers coming into Iraq. No troops had yet entered the country. And I saw Pastor Thomas returning to Baghdad, and I saw the new church. Then I saw many people coming to Jesus Christ."

Joseph lived to see every detail of his vision come to pass. And today he serves as youth leader for the Alliance Church.

"We now have about one hundred seventy young people in the youth group. Until recently, ninety-nine-point-nine percent were NOT yet born again believers. They came to the church with many problems. Sexual problems, problems with bitterness, health and financial problems. Now, these problems are coming to the surface and can be dealt with. The youth have the freedom to express themselves without fear, to talk about their inner problems which had been suppressed and hidden under the regime. Saddam is no longer in power, but Satan is still here. Most of these kids lost the ability to love; they do not understand the meaning of love.

"We had some boys who were bodybuilders. They portrayed themselves as big and tough. But when I told one young bodybuilder, 'I love you,' he started to cry. He said that even his mother has never told him she loves him. Most of this is the result of the regime and the work of the devil in Iraq.

"Under Saddam, young people lived in fear because the youth were forced into military service [military service was mandatory for men between the ages of eighteen and fifty-five]. Most of the young people worked hard at various jobs to raise enough money to buy their way out of the army [an option available only near the end of the regime]. Under Saddam, you either had to serve in the army or you had to pay a certain amount of money to be released. But the bribe was US$600 (about 1.8 million Iraqi dinar at that time), and very few could get their hands on so much money. That's how desperate the students were.

"In addition, there was a special bitterness between Saddam's sons and the youth in Iraq, especially successful young people, whether they had succeeded in sports or education or cultural enterprises. They became targets for Saddam's sons. They were monitored and interrogated and suffered other covert forms of persecution.

"So we have accepted these young people as they are. We listen to them and give them hope. We show them the love of Jesus, the freedom of Jesus, the real peace and truth of Jesus. And after only three months, thirty-five percent of these young people ARE born again.

"I believe that these young people will be the starting point for the new Iraq.

"All of them have talents. Some have the talent to sing or to act or for social services or teaching. My passion is to help each young person to identify his or her talents and gifts and make the church look like a big hospital for spiritual healing—like professional hospitals that have sections and departments and areas of specialization—and plug in these young people so that they can develop their gifts and use them to minister to the church and the community for the glory of God."

Months after the soldiers came and Pastor Thomas returned and the congregation was in its newly-furnished church building, Joseph had another vision.

"I saw a map of Iraq. It was all red,. And I knew that all of Iraq will be washed with Jesus' blood. I may not live to see it happen, but God has already fulfilled the first things that he showed to me. So I have hope that what he showed me afterward will happen as well."

* * *

IRAQI MUSLIMS URGE END TO ANTI-CHRISTIAN VIOLENCE

Stefan J. Bos, Special Correspondent, ASSIST News Service

BAGHDAD, IRAQ (ANS) Thursday, January 15, 2004—A group of politicians and intellectuals is urging Iraq's authorities, including Muslim leaders, the U.S. backed Iraqi Governing Council, and the American-led coalition, to prevent "Shi'a Muslim groups attacking Christians."

In a statement released by Barnabas Fund which monitors religious persecution, over two hundred mainly Muslim intellectuals and political leaders urged officials to stop "attacks on Christians and cease forcing women to wear the veil."

The group also urged Islamic religious leaders to issue fatwas forbidding such "atrocious crimes against humanity."

"Christians lived in Iraq for two thousand years and contributed greatly to the region's civilization, both before and after the coming of Islam," they said.

Iraqi church leaders also have been speaking out against increasing persecution. They claim missiles were launched against a convent last October and that Christians have received death threats, causing many to flee from Basra.

Church officials warn that American intervention is the only way to ensure that legislation based on Islamic law is not enacted that will cause even more Christian suffering.

But Barnabas Fund warns that the Iraqi Governing Council has nearly finalized a transitional constitution that would establish Islam as one source of its laws.

Chapter Twelve

The Presbyterian National Church in Iraq was founded in Mosul in 1840 and now has four more congregations in Baghdad, Basra, and Kirkuk.

Ikram Ibrahim leads the Evangelical Presbyterian Church in Baghdad. An Egyptian, Pastor Ikram graduated from the seminary in Cairo in 1972, ministered in Egypt for a quarter century, and came to Iraq in 1998.

Nearly fifteen hundred people attend his congregation. Most came from the historical churches after accepting Jesus as their personal Lord and Savior.

Today, Pastor Ibrahim says, many Muslims are coming to faith in Christ.

"Once I met with Trans World Radio that broadcasts Christian programming into Arabic-speaking countries like Iraq. They told me that five thousand Muslims in Iraq have contacted them, asking for Bibles and other Christian literature. And they asked me if I would allow these Muslims to come to my office at the church to talk with me about the Lord or to receive counseling. I said, yes, definitely.

"Many already have come to me, saying they had received Bibles and Christian literature. And now, with the country more open, I hope and expect that many more will come to know the Lord."

It is very dangerous for Muslim Christian families in the Evangelical Presbyterian Church. Nevertheless, they attend openly.

“Any Muslim who accepts Christ as his personal Lord and Savior can be harmed by their families or by Islamic fundamentalists, and the church is placed in danger also.

“As a church, we are open to everybody, so when Muslims come to the church, we cannot send them away. We pray for the protection of God. We do not, however, go out and overtly preach to Muslims or try to convert them. If they come to us and ask for a Bible or particular books or want to talk with us about what we believe, we do not turn them away or refuse them.

Nor do the Muslim Christians hide their relationship with Jesus by coming late, sitting in the back, or leaving early.

“They are grateful for and proud of what Jesus has done for them. They often sit in the front and wait after the service to shake hands with me.

“One time, a Muslim came to me and told me, ‘I saw Jesus Christ in a dream, and he was so glorious. So I want to know more information about him.’

“While I was answering his questions, a Muslim Christian came to the church, a man I had baptized.

“So I let them sit together, and I told the Muslim seeker that this baptized Muslim Christian can answer all your questions. Ask him, and he will tell you what he has experienced.”

* * *

VIOLENCE AGAINST CHRISTIANS AND AMERICANS SPREADS

Stefan J. Bos, Special Correspondent, ASSIST News Service

BAGHDAD, IRAQ (ANS) Wednesday, January 21, 2004 Four Christian women were killed and five others injured when militants in a passing car raked their minibus with gunfire 80 kilometers (50 miles) west of Baghdad, according to Barnabas Fund, an informed human rights watchdog group.

The group said the attack happened as nine Christian Iraqi women were on their way to work in the laundry at the Habaniyah American military base.

"Suddenly four masked men in a white Opel machine-gunned our minibus and four women died," forty-nine-year-old survivor Maggi Aziz explained from her hospital bed.

None of the passengers escaped without injuries. Aziz suffered wounds to her leg, shoulder, and head.

Among those killed was Ashkik Varojan, who boarded the bus on Wednesday morning, intending to hand in her resignation rather than live in fear of reprisals for cooperating with the United States-led coalition.

Necessity had forced her to work to support her paralyzed husband and four children.

Another survivor, Vera Ibrahim, said that she will not continue her work.

“I am afraid. They wanted to kill us all,” she said.

There was no immediate claim of responsibility,

although church leaders, individual Christians, and human rights workers have told ASSIST

News Service (ANS) in Iraq they are concerned about rising violence against Christians.

Survivor Suzanne Azat and Mussa Adam Abu Shaba, whose sister Nadia was killed, said they believe the assailants were insurgents fighting against coalition forces with whom Muslim militants often identify Iraq's Christian minority.

Human rights workers told ANS there is growing pressure on Christians to adhere to the rules of Iraq's Muslim Shi'ite majority. In cities like Basra, for example, Christian women are being threatened and some killed for refusing to wear veils.

One Basra source told Barnabas Fund of anti-American demonstrators, led by Shi'ite leader Grand Ayatollah Ali Al-Sistani, carrying pictures of Jesus.

The watchdog group said the demonstrators were trying to make it appear that Christians were supporting the Shi'ite group, "although virtually all Christian leaders" are against Al-Sistani's policies.

The Shi'ite Muslim leader is demanding direct elections before the transfer of power from the American-led coalition, and his followers have staged huge marches in support of the demand.

Despite the pressure and daily violence, Iraqi Christians risk their lives, racing through the streets in the midst of gunfire, to visit often overcrowded churches.

Chapter Thirteen

Dr. Hala Boulex grew up in the minority Armenian Church in Baghdad.

"I thought I was a good person. But when I grew older, in 1984, I saw the *Jesus Film*, and I realized for the first time that I was a sinner who needed to be saved. After I had accepted Jesus, I moved from the Armenian Church to the Evangelical Presbyterian Church and started growing in grace."

Life, however, was difficult for Christians under Saddam's corrupt regime.

"My church had lots of support from the West—donations and so forth—especially after the first Gulf crisis. But we also heard that a major part of the assistance they sent to us was being stolen by the government. I remember one time when my mom and I went shopping. We went to the store, and they were selling what was clearly Christian donations."

In addition to being victimized by the political corruption, Iraqi believers suffered basic human rights violations (see also Appendix II).

"In 1978, a large number of people in our church were put into prison because of their work of evangelism. It's totally prohibited to go and evangelize outside in the street. On the other hand, I can say there was no persecution simply because they were Christians. We had the freedom to worship our Lord in the church. But you can never go and share your faith with a Muslim. This is very dangerous.

"Another reason the people in my church were put into prison was because they were meeting together in their homes. Such meetings, like for Bible study, are not allowed. The government was suspicious of people from different cultural groups meeting together.

"Among Muslims, the Sunni meet only with Sunni, Shi'a with Shi'a, etc. Sometimes we would meet with foreigners, and Saddam's police wanted to know why people from Germany and the United States and other countries were meeting in houses with these Iraqi Christians. They decided that it was probably something political. So our brothers and sisters were humiliated and tortured and questioned and questioned. Finally, when they found out that it was purely religious, they set them free. One of my dearest friends suffered from that."

Ironically, while Baath Party government officials did all they could bureaucratically to make life difficult for Iraqi Christians, Saddam himself seemed personally friendly with them.

"Saddam trusted Christians, and most of the people who worked in his palaces were Christians—both nominal and evangelical. He wouldn't allow a Muslim to enter his bedroom or fix his breakfast for him. All those with the most intimate access to him had to be Christians. When I had my clinic in Jordan, an Assyrian lady was cleaning the clinic for me. She had worked in Saddam's palace before. She said he trusted only Christian people. In fact, when you enter the Evangelical Presbyterian Church building in Baghdad today, you will see a very great keyboard organ—it was a gift from Saddam."

While Christians suffered no overt persecution from the government, they were, and continue to be, openly and violently persecuted by the communities that surround them.

"Persecution because of someone's Christian faith came only from the Muslims. They say, 'You're just like Bush! You are spies for America! They call us collaborators and Zionists because of America's support for Israel."

But Christians were not the only ones to suffer under the former regime. With Saddam in power, no one was safe.

"Lots of people, including our neighbors, suffered torture and most of them were innocent. They just disappeared, and no one knew where they went, just because they said a joke about Saddam. They would just disappear."

And the ever-deteriorating economy caused additional suffering and frustrations.

"Medical doctors working in hospitals in and around Baghdad had to deal with many struggles and pressures and restrictions. We worked long hours and got nothing. The pay was insulting. One or two dollars a day. We worked hard to become medical doctors and then we saw all the good salaries and benefits going to the military. They had nice houses, cars, and everything else, while the workers and professionals could barely pay rent."

In 1991, Dr. Boulex left her beloved Iraq. She planned to go to the United States, where her father lives, to complete her post-graduate studies. But when she stopped over in Jordan, she met and married her husband, George, and they started a family. Later, they moved to Lebanon.

"My kids go to a very good school there. It is a good opportunity for them. But I definitely want to come back to Iraq. And I praise the Lord that he used George Bush as a part of his plan to open the door for the gospel and to liberate the people.

"Most, if not all, of the Christian people in Iraq are very, very happy that you got rid of Saddam and very grateful for what America did. And we feel so ashamed and embarrassed about what the Iraqi resistance is doing now. Rather than showing their gratitude, they are terrorizing the coalition and Iraq."

But Hala and other Iraqi Christians did not always see things this way. It took time to believe that God would bring anything good out of the horror and bloodshed.

"During the first Gulf crisis, we felt alone and very bad because America was shooting and hitting Iraq. People lived in the bomb shelters. I was helping the wounded, and we felt the rage—not only against the Americans but against us, the Christians. The Muslims started calling us Crusaders and vented their anger against us.

"But that war turned out to be a great source of blessing for the Iraqi people. It caused millions to flee. And many went to Jordan and remained there for many years and were converted, because there is a lot of religious freedom in Jordan. So I consider the first Gulf war as the beginning and the recent Gulf War as a continuation of God's plan for Iraq."

Now that the regime has fallen, the Church is free to be the Church. Free to grow and mature, to be blessed and to be a blessing.

"There were no seminaries in Iraq. Iraqi people had to study the Bible outside, mostly in Lebanon or Jordan. And now, as a result of the second Gulf crisis, they are coming back and we are getting our first Iraqi pastors (like Pastor Thomas). Before that, pastors were Egyptian or Lebanese. A few stayed, but most others came for a short time and left. If these new Iraqi pastors had returned when Saddam was still in power, it would have been very difficult for them. Now, they are free to start new churches and follow the Lord.."

* * *

AT LEAST 12 KILLED IN BOMB EXPLOSIONS IN IRAQ

Stefan J. Bos, Special Correspondent, ASSIST News Service

MOSUL, IRAQ (ANS) Saturday, January 31, 2004 -- A car bomb exploded in Mosul today, killing at least nine people. At the same time, three United States soldiers died when a roadside blast ripped through their convoy near Kirkuk, adding to fears among the local Christian population.

The attack at the main police station in Mosul, which hospital sources said also wounded forty-five people, came as Christians in the area contemplated their options following several other Muslim attacks.

Iraq's Christians have been threatened by militants who see them as supporters of the American-led coalition and Western colonial powers.

Christian students and families have received notes to convert to Islam or die.

Last November, Ismail Youssef, a prominent Christian judge, was assassinated outside his Mosul home. Several days later, authorities reportedly defused a cluster of bombs found at two Christian schools, one in Mosul and another in Baghdad.

The violence has been linked mainly to Muslim militants, including remnants of the old regime and insurgents from neighboring countries who oppose the American-coalition and a more open society that would be tolerant to other faiths, including Christianity.

It comes amid reports that a radical Islamic movement, is rapidly spreading across the troubled nation, ahead of Washington's efforts to create a more permanent multi-ethnic government and a new constitution for Iraq.

An Iraqi Christian woman, identified as Eman, told Christian Broadcasting Network (CBN) how recently a group of Muslim men ordered her to cover her head.

“They told me that if I didn't put on a veil, they would slaughter me. Can you imagine this?”

Human rights organizations say these are not isolated incidents, and there are concerns that latest developments will increase the number of Christian refugees. Since the end of the first Gulf

War, the Christian population of Iraq has dropped from nearly two million to less than a million.

CBN quoted Noah Feldman, a close adviser to American administrator Paul Bremer, as telling British media that he fears Iraq is bound to embrace Sharia, a harsh form of Islamic law, as the basis of its constitution.

Chapter Fourteen

Younan Shiba, pastor of the Assyrian Evangelical Church, lives in Baghdad with his wife, Lela, and their two daughters—six-year-old Joy and three-year-old Grace. He was born and raised in Kirkuk in northern Iraq and served in the military during the war with Iran and in the first Gulf war.

"Growing up, I was part of the Assyrian Orthodox Church and very far from the Lord. My sister became a believer in Jesus Christ and joined the Assyrian Evangelical Church. We were taught that this church belonged to the Zionists. My sister kept encouraging me to come to Christ and join her, but I told her I could never believe what she believed.

"I studied the Bible, just so I could argue with her and prove to her that she was wrong. But Scripture is like a sword, and God turned his sword against me and began to cut away the lies I believed. Soon, I realized that I was a sinner and far away from God.

"One day, in 1990, I entered my sister's church. I saw a number of young people on their knees, praying. They took turns praying until it was my turn. The leader asked me to pray. He spoke Assyrian, and that language touched my heart. He said Christ is in our midst. So I pretended to pray, repeating some Scripture verses I had memorized to use against my sister. Suddenly, I began to cry, and I lay on my face and I screamed, *God, I have been looking for you! Save me!*

"I didn't understand what salvation was at that time, but something in my heart was asking for it. So I prayed with all my heart. I felt like I was flying. And I dedicated my life to Christ. I love Jesus, because he loved me first.

"After that, I married Lela. Then I was invited to study in Jordan. Lela and I went there, and I studied for seven-and-a-half years at which time God led me to serve here in Iraq. I said, *God, I am your servant. Use me as you wish.*"

The Lord took him at his word.

During his time in Jordan, Younan pastored the Iraqi congregation in Amman and planted six other churches for Iraqi refugees. He founded a computer company and a cultural center to teach computer skills and embroidery to Iraqi refugees to enable them to support themselves.

Today, his creative ministry continues in his homeland.

Younan serves as the head of the Assyrian Evangelical Denomination and as pastor of the Baghdad church. As he had done in Jordan, he launched a nongovernment organization (NGO) called the Mesopotamia Society for Community Development. Recently, Pastor Younan planted a second church, which now serves six hundred people in south Baghdad. And he has contracted to open a new NGO, called Salt, which will house a computer training and cultural center.

What does he see as he looks to the future?

"God is opening doors, especially in the north of Iraq—very old and tightly shut doors.

The keys have been lost for thirty-five years, but God does not need keys. However, those doors may not remain open. No one knows when they might close again after the new government is in place. So I need to seize the opportunity while it is there. Many Iraqis—participants in the ancient Sunni/Shiite conflict and members of the Iraqi resistance—are working against Iraq. But the children of God must work together to save Iraq. We must begin quickly, because we do not know what will happen tomorrow.

"We feel the hand of the Lord working among us. He has protected the church so far. We are very poor, but we are starting to train and teach and empower the people by starting seminaries and training centers. First, though, they must be healed and strengthened—body, soul and spirit."

* * *

Nashwan Necola supports Pastor Younan as assistant pastor. He was led to Christ in 1985 by his persistent brother-in-law. He studied theology in Lebanon and returned to Iraq in 1995, where he served as a teaching pastor for a year. Then Nashwan became senior pastor of the Assyrian Evangelical Church, which he led until Pastor Younan arrived. Today, he serves as assistant pastor while continuing his theological studies through the internet and working toward his doctorate degree.

The Assyrian Evangelical Church was founded by a Presbyterian American missionary who came to Iraq from Iran. He bought a tract of land and opened a private Christian school in 1920 and a church building the following year. The students were taught Aramaic and about Christianity, in addition to their regular school subjects.

From 1950, when the founder died, to 1995 several Assyrians pastored the church, but each stayed for only a short time and left. And during the thirty years between 1965 and 1995, there was no regular pastor at all.

"Another Egyptian pastor served in the Presbyterian church before Pastor Ikram, and he used to conduct prayer meetings every Friday for the remaining members of the Assyrian Church. So most of the members of the Assyrian church left and emigrated to the United States.

"When I became the pastor, only eight to ten people remained. I do not have an Assyrian background, but I restarted the ministry for this small church, and my wife started a Sunday school with just five children—our two daughters and several other children in the church. Over the past eight years, many Assyrian families began to return. And many others from the historical Assyrian church have accepted the Lord and now worship here."

Saddam's Ministry of Religious Affairs paid particularly close attention to this church during the former regime. Sunday meetings were monitored, Nashwan recalls, and he believes that he was followed, probably because he had studied in a Baptist seminary.

"The government was particularly suspicious of anything Baptist because of the link it believed the Baptists had to President Bush."

The biggest difficulty, though, was the loss of their school. The government nationalized it, turned it into a government school and buried the church in a mountain of red tape when it tried to get the school back.

Because of the danger of meeting with foreigners, Nashwan avoided them, "even just to say hello, because if you were seen talking to a foreigner, the next day a government officer would come and question you or begin to follow you to see what you were up to.

"If you had foreigners come to your church for any reason, the Religious Affairs Ministry was to be notified. Many times, I was afraid that the knock on the door might be a squad from the government to arrest me and put me in prison. No house, no person in Iraq, was safe. If they wanted to arrest you or to hang you, they could do it. There was no one to stop them. So the only way to live was to trust God.

"Paul said, 'If we live, we live to the Lord; and if we die, we die to the Lord. So, whether we live or die, we belong to the Lord.'[88] I believe that. We used to pray, 'God, we know you are here and we trust you, and our life is yours. Please protect us and steer our life in the way that you want to.' That is the only way to survive. There are no other people, no organizations, no countries to trust. Only God."

---

[88] 'Romans 14:8.

Despite the fact that Iraqis had no access to world news, and satellite dishes were not allowed, the early months of 2003 carried rumors about another war. And they were very afraid.

"We prayed that God would protect Iraq from war, but we knew deep in our hearts that it was coming.

"When the war began, some of us climbed up to the roof. We could see the huge Cruise Missiles pass over our heads on their way toward the government buildings. One time, we counted up to fifty missiles. Ten hit nearby at the air force base. The explosions were very strong and shook our houses. It felt like they were swinging.

"After the bombing stopped, we drove around the city and could hear much shooting. Soon, we saw the tanks thundering down the street next to ours.

"Today, we are filled with mixed feelings, between fear and joy. We are happy to get rid of thirty years of fear. But now we are afraid again—everybody, not just Christians—because the situation here is so unstable and uncertain. We are insecure, and the living situation is very difficult.

"The Americans made hundreds of promises, but nothing has happened. They made some mistakes, like dismissing the Iraqi army. The situation might be better now if the Americans had just paid the soldiers' salaries and left them in place to keep us safe.

"In addition to the fears and uncertainties, we have many people in our church with no jobs, and this causes more problems for everybody. Our congregation is very poor."

Nashwan and his family often helped these families out of their own pockets and went without. Sometimes his family went into debt, borrowing money to help someone in need.

Everything is available today in the marketplaces, but prices are very high—much too expensive for the daily workers, carpenters, plumbers, drivers, and others in his church, because there is no demand now for their kind of work. Even those who have government jobs and receive decent salaries cannot keep up with the soaring cost of living.

But there is good news too.

"God's Word is coming to the surface, and people are very thirsty. We had to stop services during the war. So we went from house to house to minister to the families. Sometimes my wife and I would have to run for shelter until the bombing stopped. But since the collapse of the regime, the church doors are open and many new people have come."

So many people, Nashwan says, that they are already planting two new congregations—one in Aldora, ten kilometers away and another in Mosul.

But the vision of the Assyrian Evangelical Church extends past the boundaries of Iraq and out to the nations.

"God has just blessed this country," says Nashwan. "And whenever God's blesses a country, any country, that country will be a blessing to others. When God's peace filled my heart, I was blessed and, as a , I have become a blessing for other people. This does not mean that persecution and more difficulty will not come. Jesus said, 'if anyone would come after me, he must deny himself and take up his cross and follow me. For whoever wants to save his life will lose it, but whoever loses his life for me will find it.'[89]

"'I have told you these things,' the Lord said, 'so that in me you may have peace. In this world you will have trouble. But take heart! I have overcome the world.'"[90]

* * *

ASSYRIAN CHRISTIANS CRY FOR HELP

Stefan J. Bos, Special Correspondent, ASSIST News Service

FALLUJAH, IRAQ (ANS) Saturday, February 14, 2004—At least twenty-one people were killed and many others wounded today in Iraq's tense Sunni triangle, shortly after the country's Assyrian Christian community warned its churches that they will become the next target of a terrorism.

Voice of America (VOA) said the attackers fired rocket-propelled grenades and automatic weapons at the police station in a daring attack on a police compound.

The latest violence, which followed two suicide blasts this week that killed over one hundred people, underscored concern, especially among minority Christians, about what they see as Muslim violence against them and those supporting the American-led coalition. Several Assyrian Christian churches have already

[89] Matthew 16:24-25.
[90] John 16:33.

received threatening letters and leaflets, Radio Free Europe/Radio Liberty (RFE/RL) reported. And many churches are responding by working only during daylight hours, cutting back the number of services, and changing their meeting times.

But some Iraqi Muslim organizations denied threatening Christians. An official of Al-Hawza al-Ilmia, a powerful Shi'a movement, said his group condemns unconditionally the threats against the Christian churches.

"We heard about the signs that [Christian churches] might be attacked, and we condemn such operations, because Islam respects all sacred places, like mosques, churches, et cetera," said Sheikh Abd al-Jabbar Menhal, a Baghdad representative of the group.

Chapter Fifteen

Iraq is home to about twelve thousand Syrian Catholic families, which by Iraqi reckoning translates into more than seventy thousand people. Eleven hundred of those families attend St. Joseph Syrian Catholic Church in Baghdad, pastored by Byos Qasha.

Monsignor Qasha was born in 1953 in a small Christian village outside of Mosul. He was ordained twenty years later and came to pastor this church a decade after that.

"When I arrived, there were only ten people in the congregation. So I started visiting each family in their homes and got to know them. By 1993, God had blessed and expanded the church so much that there was not enough room for them all to fit into the building. So we built a bigger one, despite our poverty during the embargo."

Monsignor Qasha is also a prolific writer with fifty-two books to his credit and a magazine that he launched in 1996. He's in bed by 8:30 and up at 4:00 to pray and study and write. Daytime is devoted to ministry and evening to family visitations.

Those personal relationships were critical during the war.

"On the night before the bombing started, I had a vision from the Lord, and I told my people not to panic because God will secure us very quickly from this war."

But it was difficult to hold onto the vision in the midst of the thunder and blood and fire.

"Along with the youth in our church, we went around during the bombing, visiting the church and bringing them food and supplies, and praying with them and encouraging them. About twenty families were forced to flee their homes, and we took care of them for a week here in the church hall."

Suddenly, the bombing stopped, just as the Lord had promised.

"We held a special meeting and spent the entire time thanking God for ending the war and keeping us safe."

Now the regime is crushed. Iraq has an opportunity to be reborn. And Monsignor Qasha's eyes are fixed on where the Lord will lead next.

"I am very optimistic about the future, even though circumstances now are very difficult. Iraq's future now is for Jesus Christ. Jesus is saying the same thing to Christians in Iraq as he said to Peter once before, 'Come, Peter, don't be afraid.' Our burdens today are very heavy, but Jesus said that his burden is very light.

"My greatest concern and what I pray for most is that the Christians will not leave Iraq. Much Christian blood has been shed here and is still being shed here. But I pray that we will all stay here and not flee to other countries. This is the land of Abraham. And I pray that our faith will grow and go out from here to the nations around us."

To make it easier for these families to stay in Iraq, Monsignor Qasha recently launched a special discipleship program. It is aimed especially at parents to equip them to shore up and strengthen their children's faith during the very difficult circumstances since the war.

"People in Iraq and throughout the world are searching for peace, real peace. And I believe that my mission, the mission of the church in Iraq, is to bring to them God's message of true peace. Then Iraq will truly be the handiwork of God."

Chapter Sixteen

Up to now, you have heard from the Christian men of Iraq. Men with congregations to protect and nurture. Men with visions that embrace hundreds or thousands of families. But each of those families includes wives and mothers. Women with hopes and dreams and, yes, fears for their children. Women with a different perspective of life under and after Saddam.

Monsignor Qasha's wife, Elda, shares her heart freely and honestly, revealing a strength of faith that could come only from God.

"Fear was part of our life. But the main thing for us was to trust in God. And really we did. We trusted that God was putting his hands around us and protecting us and all our family and all our friends wherever they go. And we felt his hands, not only *knew* he was there but *felt* it, even in the dark days with the bombs—the bombs and the terrible, choking pollution from everything burning everywhere. There was only black smoke all around. For my children and for other children, and especially for sick people, it was a very difficult time."

Like many evangelical Christians in Iraq, Elda was raised in an historical church, unaware of what it meant to be reborn.

"When I was a little girl, my mother taught us to love Jesus. Not the right way as I know him now, but it had some effect on me. When I was growing up, about eighteen or nineteen years old, I was trying to fill the emptiness I felt.

I went to England, and I studied for three years, but whatever was empty inside me was not filled. Three months after I returned to Iraq, my cousin told me that there was a new church. She said, 'Come with me, and you will be filled.'

"I went there, and I heard what the pastor was saying. I couldn't stop going to the church. And little by little, I understood why. Because I loved Jesus. I thank the Lord that, even when I was a teenager and didn't really know him, God protected me."

And what about her own two daughters, now sixteen and seventeen years old? What was it like for them under the former regime?

"When our daughters were children, we didn't even speak about Saddam and these things in front of them. We tried to raise them as just ordinary children. They had lots of questions about the things the school made them learn and write and say about the regime. And we just said, this is what the school wants, so you have to say it. But when they grew up, they felt that there was something not normal.

"The year before the war, we went to Jordan where they saw the freedom, and they saw other teenagers with their minds so open. And my daughters realized that their lives were not like these teenagers. They saw that they did not know half of the things that the rest of the world knows. When they came back, they said, 'Why are we so backward? Why don't we have what they have?' And we said that God's will shall be done. Maybe today is not God's time; tomorrow it will be his time.

"We just kept putting everything in God's hands. Because the day we came to Jesus, even before I got married, I said my life belongs to Jesus and my family will be in Jesus' hands. If he wants us here in Iraq, then there is work for us to do here. If he wants us to go to another place, then there is work there that we will do for his glory. The world is just a place that we live in for a number of years, and we are just visitors. This is not our real life; our life is after this. And our aim here is to preach and to share the gospel. For us now, God wants us in Baghdad."

Elda not only supports her husband's ministry but also works faithfully and diligently at the work the Lord has given to her.

"I have a very deep trust in God, and we take our trust and faith and love to other mothers and other families and counsel them and encourage them to trust God as we do. We pray with them to give them strength and tell them that the Lord is with us. His hand is with us. His angels surround us.

"There came a time when all of us were afraid. All our children were required to become members of the regime's Baath Party. Any children who refused were removed from school. And we knew that, if they had no education, they had no future. That was very difficult for all the mothers. We prayed that this situation would not come to our children.

"But it did.

"One day our children were asked to sign papers to become members of the regime. We pleaded with the teachers and government authorities, but they refused us. We told them that they are just children. Why can't they be allowed to grow up freely and then when they are over eighteen, let them decide for themselves? But they refused. Thank God that all the papers are burned up now! Everything got burned up in the war.

"We prayed for God to change Saddam's heart or do something, because our children were growing up in a country that was becoming more and more difficult for them to live. We didn't know what else to do, so we put our children in front of the Lord, and he answered us."

* * *

IRAQ: ADVANCING TIDE OF ISLAMISATION

By Elizabeth Kendal,
World Evangelical Alliance Religious Liberty Commission
Special to ASSIST News Service

AUSTRALIA (ANS) Wednesday, February 11, 2004—Iraqi lawyers and staff advisers to the American-led Coalition Provisional Authority (CPA) are working on Iraq's Transitional Administrative Law in consultation with members of the Iraqi Governing Council (IGC). This law is a key document in the process of establishing Iraq's new constitutional order. It is therefore most concerning that it fails to guarantee full religious freedom to all.

Non-Muslims will have a limited freedom of religious practice, Muslims will still not have freedom to convert, and Islam will be privileged as the official state religion. A Shi'a majority control the US-appointed Iraqi Governing Council (IGC), and Shi'a religious leader Grand Ayatollah

Ali Al-Sistani wields great influence over the Iraqi Shi'a majority. Iraq really is at a critical juncture. Islam has been liberated and Islamisation is sweeping over the country like an advancing tide.

The IGC has already voted to replace Iraq's civil family law with Islamic sharia law, a move that will discriminate against women and Christians in child custody matters. For example: if an Iraqi Christian man converted to Islam, his Christian wife would be divorced and she would lose custody of her children who would be officially decreed to be Muslim (and 'conversion' to Christianity would be apostasy). Exactly this happened to a young Mandaean girl under Saddam Hussein while he was uniting Iraq under Islam after the first Gulf War. (Mandaeans are followers of John the Baptist.) When she came of age she courageously petitioned the Iraqi courts to change her religious identity back to Mandaean. She lost her case and fled for her life.

Around 2.5 percent of Iraqis are Christian: Arab and Kurdish evangelicals, Armenian Apostolic, Chaldean Church of Babylon, Syrian Orthodox, Presbyterian, Assyrian Church of the East (founded in northwest Iraq in 33 A.D.), and others. Iraq is very unstable: Shi'a against Shi'a, Sunni against Shi'a, Arabs and Kurds against each other, Islamists against everybody. Evidence has emerged of a Sunni Islamist plan to incite a sectarian war to draw more Sunni jihadis into Iraq. Tribal courts are operating on Islamic principles in Basra. Orthodox Islamic law leaves Christians extremely vulnerable as their testimony is virtually worthless in court and their lives count for very little, making them ideal targets for those with criminal or hateful intent.

Chapter Seventeen

Whether Christians in Iraq were openly persecuted during Saddam's reign depends upon whom you ask.

When the government took the school in which Armenian children had been taught since 1858, Father Azizian, pastor of the Armenian Orthodox Church, considered it to be persecution.

"It was religious prejudice against Christians, not racial prejudice against Armenians. They did this to all Christian schools."

Whatever the motive, it hurt.

Father Azizian was born in Baghdad in 1960. His grandfather came from Iran in 1918 after the Armenian genocide, and he lived in Kirkuk, Mosul, and Baghdad. His father was born in Baghdad; his mother came from Russia in 1946.

Father Azizian served in the Iraqi Army for twelve years, which included the war with Iran.

"I never killed anyone. Because my family was from Iran, the government did not trust me to be on the front lines. So they put me in the Kurdish mountains, very far away in the north, where we lost many men to the cold."

He was ordained in 1988 and served a church in Kirkuk for the next nine years. Since then, he has pastored the Armenian Orthodox Church in Baghdad and ministered to its seven hundred families. He and his wife, Silva, have three daughters—five, thirteen, and seventeen.

Schools nationalized by the government back in 1972 are a big issue today among the historical churches. They want them back, as well as the land on which they sit.

"Our school was mixed, boys and girls. The first thing the government did when they took it over was to separate the boys from the girls. Then they brought in students from the worst school in Baghdad. Finally, they closed the high school and secondary classes.

"It all began when government officials came and said they wanted to rent the school building and turn it into a government school 'for the good of the community.'

"In other cases, they 'bought' the school buildings and the land, paying only a fraction of the worth of the buildings and giving the church a tract of useless land very far away in exchange for the school land."

That would have been bad enough. But it didn't stop there.

"Once the government took over the Christian schools, they tried to get the Christian students to attend Islamic classes. It was not law. But the school advisers were members of the Baath Socialist Party, and they tried to manipulate the students. If, however, the teachers and students resisted strongly, the students did not have to attend."

On the record, Saddam Hussein did not harass the churches. But it was a case of the right hand pretending that it did not know what the left hand was doing—the right hand being Saddam and the left hand being his Baath bureaucrats. Harassment and intimidation was by rules and regulations rather than by law. Even though Saddam's mouth sometimes spoke against Baath activities, his head still nodded and his hands still handed them money. Everyone knew that no one did anything in Iraq unless a) Saddam knew about it and, b) Saddam approved.

"The law said that, if at least 25 percent of the students in a school were Christian, the school had to teach classes in Christianity. But the administrators got around the law by manipulating the figures to show that there were fewer than 25 percent, even if there were more. Or, instead of simply lying about the figures, they limited the Christian 'quota' to less than 25 percent and would not allow more Christians into the school."

Like most other Iraqi pastors, Father Azizian is concerned that some of his people will leave unless things improve very soon.

"We need to comfort our congregation and help the families heal. We encourage them not to leave, to stay and help to rebuild. There will be jobs again, and salaries will once again be more than two or three dollars a day. Now that Saddam is gone, we can teach in our churches what we really believe in our hearts and not be afraid of spies and what they will tell the government. We have hope that we will be able to get back our buildings and land and re-open our schools. There is a future for Iraq."

Chapter Eighteen

Apart from their spiritual kinship with one another, most Christians in Iraq have a distinct ethnic identity that, while it may not be divisive, says clearly, "I am not quite like you."

They also have very long memories, rooted deeply in their histories, a characteristic difficult for the Westerner to get his head around.

Father Nadheer Dakko, for example, is a Chaldean, born in the north around Mosul. His Mother of Sorrows Catholic Church in Baghdad ministers to around five thousand people.

To understand him and our Chaldean brothers and sisters, we need to understand a little of their ethnic identity and recent history, which they are always eager to share to an attentive ear. Father Dakko is no exception.

"In the north, in the war against Iran, Saddam moved the Chaldean Christians out of more than thirty-five of our villages, relocating us to cities like Mosul.

"Then he ordered the villages, including a nine-hundred-year-old church, to be bombed. He explained that because the villages were so close to the Iranian border, he did this to 'protect' them. Thousands of families lost everything they owned—land, houses, livestock. Everything. And the government paid them a very small token amount to cover their losses.

"When the Chaldean Christians reached the cities, Saddam ordered all the men to leave their wives and children, with little or no support, and go into the army. Many of those men were killed, and nobody seemed to care.

"Nobody even knows how many Christians died in that war.

"Also, during the war with Iran, the government ordered the creation of an all-Christian army, a Malko army, who were sent to defend the northern villages. One day, there was a big battle between Iran and Iraq. They sent the Malko army to the front lines, and the Iraqi-ordered bombing 'accidentally' killed countless Chaldean Christians.

"As a result, we have many families without husbands and fathers. The single mothers are forced to go out of the home to work. The schools hate the Christian children and treat them badly.

"In 1972, the Christian schools were nationalized by the government, which also mandated that the Koran was to be taught in the schools, even to Christians.

"But the Chaldean Christian families refused to allow their children to study the Koran. The Patriarch went to Saddam and asked that the Chaldean children be excused. The government stopped the Koran lessons, but then they put Koranic verses in the textbooks of all the other subjects, even in the science books. So it appeared that the Chaldean children were not actually studying the Koran, but they had to memorize religious verses and learn only about the history of Iraq and Islam, not any Chaldean, Christian, or Assyrian history.

"Many of the children left the schools. But it is shameful in the Oriental culture for the mother to be working and a twelve-year-old 'man' to be in the house. So these children went out and got menial jobs cleaning shoes or herding goats in order to keep their mothers home and support their families.

"Today, many Chaldean Christian youth do not have enough education. They cannot even write Arabic. Chaldean Christians used to have excellent educations and were the architects and doctors and scientists.

"Then, after the first Gulf War, Saddam opened the borders for Christians to flee. And many—especially the most qualified, the best-educated, and professionals—who had been living such a hard life and just wanted a decent life, left Iraq and fled to France and the U.S., Australia, New Zealand, Sweden, and so on. And this was the plan of the government, but it was 'under the table,' not open persecution. A doctor, a full professor of physics or chemistry, was paid less than $50 per month. And rent alone on a house was more than $50 a month. I had a house in the north, but they bombed my village, and I can barely rent a house in Baghdad now."

The wounds are deep, the challenges daunting for Iraqi Christians.

"I am a priest, and I haven't enough education to solve all of these problems. I haven't enough power to take care of everything. But I believe in my God, and we hope."

Chapter Nineteen

"The church in Iraq is very strong," declares Rev. Ashraf Mossa Mehanni, pastor of the Evangelical Presbyterian Church in Mosul "The faith of the Christians is very strong after what they have endured under Saddam."

Pastor Ashraf believes that God used Saddam's reign of terror to strengthen the church in Iraq, a powerful reminder "that in all things God works for the good of those who love him, who have been called according to his purpose."[91]

And that makes Ashraf extremely optimistic and enthusiastic about the future of his adopted country.

An Egyptian, he came to Christ when he heard an evangelistic message in a worship service in Cairo.

"I heard Jesus call me by name to serve him. Even with that, it was a difficult decision to come to Iraq. For ten years, the church had no resident pastor because of the bad conditions here. During that time, another Egyptian pastor working in Kirkuk came here to Mosul every other Friday and preached. But finally, he returned to Egypt. After 1999, the church had no pastor at all until I arrived immediately after the second Gulf War."

Today, every service in the century-and-a-half-old church building is filled to the doors.

And many more want to come but cannot

[91] Romans 8:28.

because the church is in a bad location and they are unable to reach it.

But this congregation has been faithful with what God has put into its hands, including a medical clinic among its community outreaches. And recently God gave it more.

"The government recently donated a large tract of land, and we are going to build a new church, a hospital, and maybe a Christian school. This would have been impossible under Saddam. Back then, the Religious Affairs Ministry even determined the maximum number of families that were allowed in each church.

"In addition to the land, the Lord gave me a badly-needed vehicle, so that I can minister to our families and to others in the community."

Pastor Ashraf is excited about the new freedom he and other Christians are experiencing.

"God is doing such wonderful things in Iraq today. Now, if someone asks me a question about Jesus, I can answer freely. Recently, a Kurdish man asked me for a Bible, and I was free to give him one. These things were not possible under Saddam. Now we are free to have satellite dishes. These were forbidden before. So people can now receive religious broadcasts and hear about Jesus. And Christians can be taught and strengthen their faith and learn more about how to share it with others. Now, the doors are open to foreign missionaries, and we are allowed to meet with them and work with them."

"And one day soon, I believe that the church in Iraq will send our own missionaries to other countries. It is time for the people of Iraq to come to Jesus Christ."

Chapter Twenty

Hilal Ghanim was nineteen years old when he came to Christ.

"I had a disease that I believed was going to kill me. I wanted to die. My heart was empty, and I was searching for something to fill it."

Obviously, the disease did not kill Hilal, nor did Iraq's deadly wars.

"In 1986, during the war with Iran, all the soldiers who had not yet fought on the front lines were ordered to move up to them, which was like a sentence of death. We had only one month before we had to go. So I prayed. At the end of that month, the government discharged everyone born in 1956. So I did not have to go to the front.

"Three months later, the government told us all to report again for military service. Again, I fasted and prayed. And just when the time came for me to go in again, the war ended.

"Once again, war came. This time it was the Gulf War against the Americans. And once again, I was called to be a soldier. My wife was terrified that I would be killed. I told her that I was in Jesus' hands. I reported to Baghdad, and they assigned me to Mosul. I was in the army here for three months. Then that war ended, and I was released again from military service."

Hilal's wife, Samar, was born in Nineveh in 1963. Like her parents, Samar knew *about* Jesus, but she did not know *him*. That day would come, but the years in between nearly destroyed both her and her marriage.

"Samar had just finished university and gained her degree when we married," Hilal recalled. "She did not know the Lord. She lived for the world. I was a deacon in the Evangelical Presbyterian Church here in Mosul. I would take her to church with me sometimes, and in the car I had a cassette player and would play Christian music. And she would say, why are we listening to this music? Put in something else. I told her, no, this recorder is for Christian music and in my car that is all you can listen to. Sometimes she threatened to throw my tape out the window, and I told her I would just bring another one.

"'How can I live with this man?' she asked her family. 'He is always in the church and always with the Bible. I want to go to the hotels and restaurants and to parties.' "

"The first year of our marriage was okay," Samar recalled. "After that, I became pregnant and gave birth to a daughter. We named her Lydia. She lived one year and became a very beautiful girl. Then there was a difficulty and our child died.

"At this time, I was pregnant with our first son. He too was very beautiful, but he lived for only seven months, and then he too died.

"For months, I cried and cried. People wanted to help us. Our Muslim neighbors said they could make magic papers for us that would give us a healthy baby. So my mother and I went secretly to get these papers. I took off the cross I had been wearing and wore the magic papers beneath my clothes."

Hilal had no idea what was happening.

"When Samar and her mother asked me to drive them to the Muslim home to get the magic papers, I did not know why they were going. Then, when we arrived, they told me to stay outside. They went in and left me outside for one hour. I asked what they were doing in there, what happened to them, and they said. 'Nothing.' "

"After I had worn the magic papers for almost one year," Samar continued, "Hilal took me to a Christian conference in Amman, Jordan. There, I met some Christian women and shared with them my problem and my grief. One of the women encouraged me to burn the magic papers.

"I was afraid. But I burned them and began to read the Bible. As the conference continued, I met a very old woman. She told me about the miracles Jesus did, and I began to feel the need for Jesus Christ in my life. As I accepted him, many brothers and sisters came and prayed for me. They put their hands on my stomach and asked the Lord to give us a child that would live.

"When we returned to Iraq, we had lost all our sadness. And our neighbors asked, 'Why are you very happy? What happened to you?'

"I told them, 'Jesus has entered my heart and changed my life. I won't listen to any of you anymore.'

"Our first two children died of Reyes Syndrome. Because the cause is unknown, the doctors in Lebanon (we had been in Lebanon taking the Great Commission Training Course) told us that it would be very dangerous to have a child and encouraged us to adopt.

"But they were wrong. And God gave us Fahdi. After that, he gave us Fahdia. And they are both beautiful and healthy."

The fear of conceiving and losing more children was over. And now, after the second Gulf war, other fears were gone as well.

"During Saddam," Hilal said, "there were many police reports written about me and questions asked about who I was and what I was doing and who I knew. And I believe that, if the regime had continued, the security car would have come and arrested me and taken me to Baghdad and put me in prison. So the first American soldier I met when the army came, I told him, 'I am praying for you to win the war.'

"We have no idea of what the future holds after Saddam Hussein," said Samar. "We have only one thing in our heart. We are children in the hands of Jesus Christ."

* * *

AMERICAN PASTOR DIES IN IRAQI AMBUSH

By Jeremy Reynalds, Special Correspondent for ASSIST News Service

BAGHDAD, IRAQ (ANS) Wednesday, February 18, 2004—The U.S. military has confirmed that gunmen killed an American pastor when the taxi he was riding in was ambushed outside Baghdad.

The Baptist Press reported that John Kelley, 48, was pastor of Curtis Corner Baptist Church, an independent Baptist church in South Kingstown, Rhode Island. He was traveling with a number of other ministers who went to Iraq on a two-week trip to explore the possibility of starting a church there.

U.S. paratroopers from the 82nd Airborne Division learned of the Feb. 14 attack while patrolling the town of Mahmudiyah, about fifteen miles south of Baghdad, according to *The Associated Press.* They were told the Americans had been riding in a taxi when a white sedan pulled up alongside and opened fire.

Three other men, including David Davis of Grace Bible Baptist Church in Vernon, Connecticut, and Kirk DiVietro of Grace Baptist Church in Franklin, Massachusetts, were injured in the ambush and were being treated at an Iraqi hospital.

Kelley, a former Marine, leaves a wife and four children. *The Boston Globe* reported that Kelley's wife, Jane, had received a bouquet of flowers her husband had arranged to be sent on Valentine's Day. Several hours later, she was told of his death.

According to *The Boston Globe* the group was a loose-knit delegation led by Pastor Robert Lewis of Cumberland, Rhode Island. Members were helping an Iraqi pastor open what they believed would be the first Baptist church in the country.

"The door is open right now. You can't wait until it's safe over there. You've got to go when there is opportunity," said Erik Vukic, a thirty-five-year-old construction worker who was serving as a spokesman for Kelley's church.

The newspaper quoted State Department spokesman Richard Boucher as saying that the administration discourages travel to Iraq by private citizens and does not encourage missionary work.

"We have a very strong travel warning that tells people not to go to Iraq, that it still remains a dangerous place," he said. Travel has been discouraged for "any Americans except for those that might be engaged in official duties or in support of the effort that's underway now."

Chapter Twenty-One

Nova Hagopian, director of the Bible Society of Iraq, is one of the many bright lights in Iraq. Born in Baghdad in 1971, he became a goldsmith. But he never touched real gold until he met Jesus.

"I was twenty years old. My mother was always asking me to come to church. 'There are many evangelists coming to Iraq,' she said. 'You have to see them. You have to accept Jesus.'

"I told her, 'Why do I need to come to Jesus? I'm a good person.'

"I went to church from time to time. Usually, I spent my free time visiting the three Armenian clubs (social clubs that promote the Armenian language, history, and culture) where I talked and drank and danced with my friends.

"One day, I was visiting the church and, after the sermon, the preacher asked who would like to come to the front and give his heart to Jesus. I ran to the front and raised my hands and said I want to be with Jesus."

Five years later, Nova went on his first trip with the Bible Society. In 2000, he joined the staff, and three years later he was named director of the Bible Society in Iraq.

"So many churches have been asking for Scriptures, and without him everything would have come to a stand-still," says Tom Hoglind, the Bible Society's distribution and information manager in Beirut, Lebanon. "God's given him strength, although he keeps on saying over the phone: ‘We're living a dog's life over here! Pray for us!’ ”

The Bible Society worked officially in Iraq until 1978 through a Bible House on a main business street. Then, on November 4, many committed Christians were arrested and imprisoned. Some were sentenced to five years. Their “crime” was meeting together in their homes. Among those arrested were two Bible Society employees—the director, Fuad Daoud, and Yousef Lahoud from the Bible Society in Lebanon. As a result, the work of the Bible Society was put on hold.

Five years later, employees of the Bible Society in Jordan started an intensive work to supply the Church of Iraq with the scriptures it needed. Since then, throughout the tyranny of Saddam Hussein, a trickle of Bibles has swelled into a flood.

“I don't think we'll ever forget some of the large shipments,” Hoglind recalls, “up to sixty tons of Scriptures arriving in Iraq.”

Conclusion

The region known today as Iraq has been home to many people groups, the birthplace of empires, and the beginning of civilization itself.

But when you sort it all out, its complex and generally bloody history has really concerned only two kinds of people—God's people and everyone else.

Charles Dickens might have described Iraq as the best and the worst. Wise and foolish. Those who believe and those who do not. Light and darkness, hope and despair, everything and nothing, "those going direct to Heaven and those going direct the other way."[92]

Those going to heaven are the only hope for those going the other way. They carry the light to show the way to those living in darkness. They carry the only true hope to those living in despair. With or without telephones, electricity, food or shelter, they have everything worth having, while everybody else has nothing worth having.

And God has called these former—these born-again believers, these Christ-followers—to be conformed to Christ, to reach their nation with the Gospel, and to carry the Lord's blessings far beyond their borders.

Scripture promises that Iraq will play a major role in the "end of days." The words of Isaiah 19:23-25 are the rallying cry, the hope, and the reward of the Church in Iraq:

---

[92] Charles Dickens, *A Tale of Two Cities*, Chapter One, 1859.

> In that day there will be a highway from Egypt to Assyria. The Assyrians will go to Egypt and the Egyptians to Assyria. The Egyptians and Assyrians will worship together. In that day Israel will be the third, along with Egypt and Assyria, a blessing on the earth. The Lord Almighty will bless them, saying, "Blessed by Egypt my people, Assyria my handiwork, and Israel my inheritance."

Egypt, the womb of the Church.
Israel, land of the covenant.
Iraq, God's handiwork.

> **handiwork** (hăn′dē-wûrk′) *n.* 1. Work performed by power and wisdom. *"The heavens declare the glory of God; and the firmament showeth his handiwork"* (Psalm xix:i KJV).[93]

How can bloody Iraq be the work of God's hands? How can God speak this way of the land that laid grisly siege to Israel and Judah and dragged off his people to cruel captivity? How can "Babylon the Great, the mother of prostitutes and the abomination of the earth" possibly be the Lord's handiwork?

Probably just as you and I—along with all the other gossips, slanderers, God-haters,

[93] Noah Webster, *American Dictionary of the English Language*, 1828.

insolent, arrogant and boastful, those who disobey their parents or who are senseless, faithless, heartless, and ruthless[94]—can be forgiven and reborn.

God loves terrorists, too. Remember the apostle Paul, who "put many of the saints in prison, and when they were put to death, I cast my vote against them. Many a time I went from one synagogue to another to have them punished, and I tried to force them to blaspheme. In my obsession against them, I even went to foreign cities to persecute them."[95]

Just as God has always had a purpose for you and me, he has always had a purpose for Iraq. And just as he will fulfill his purposes for us, he will do so for Iraq.

"The zeal of the Lord Almighty will accomplish this."[96]

Our mission is to demonstrate God's love and mercy, to reflect his glory and dispense his blessings to those around us.

Iraq's mission, along with Egypt and Israel, has always been to bless the earth.

Like the sons of Issachar, however, we must be able to read the signs of the times.[97]

Today, the Holy Spirit is moving mightily throughout the Middle East. Despite the violence and apparent chaos, he is stirring the hearts of Arab youth and fortifying their courage. He is giving them a vision for life beyond anything they have known. After

---

[94] Romans 1:30-31
[95] Acts 26:10-11
[96] 2 Kings 19:31; Isaiah 9:7; 37:32
[97] 1 Chronicles 12:32

fourteen centuries of ignorance and isolation, God is shining the light of truth and hope into the Muslim world.

By definition, you and I are involved in this amazing transformation, for when one part of the body of Christ suffers, Scripture declares, the entire body suffers with it.[98]

Christ has only one body. He is not divided. We may not physically *feel* that we share in one another's sufferings, but we do.

I can have cancer, in which the killer cells are constantly destroying my healthy cells, tissue, and systems. I may not be aware of it, but I am dying nonetheless. With many diseases, like cancer or AIDS, by the time the person realizes something is wrong, it is too late.

If I break my big toe, it may be that only my toe and the area around it hurts. Yet my whole body is thrown off balance and may even be immobilized. It affects the quality of my life, just as a wounded part of the body of Christ affects the spiritual life and effectiveness of the whole.

When our Iraqi brothers and sisters suffer, we may not feel it and the symptoms may not show for a long time before we are aware that something is wrong, but it hurts the body of Christ.

With this in mind, Paul wrote that we are to "rejoice with those who rejoice; mourn with those who mourn."[99]

After the 9/11 terrorist attacks, Ken Sehested and Kyle Childress amplified that

---

[98] 1 Corinthians 12:26

[99] Romans 12:15

verse in the following reflection, which provides an excellent guide for us all:

> At a moment like this, the first engagement of the body of Christ is to engage in the ministry of grieving. Holy grief, the practice of lament, is not a form of self-centered pity but the willingness to crouch with those forced to their knees in the face of devastation. Grieving is also a powerful antidote to the arrogance of self-sufficiency, to confidence in wishful thinking and human control. There is a sustaining force in the universe that we can trust, which is available but not manageable.
>
> The second engagement for the body of Christ is to intercede in prayer. Intercessory prayer is not a form of spiritual hocus-pocus; we have no magical wand to wave, to make the hurt go away. Intercessory prayer keeps us in a heightened state of readiness to intervene with compassion when the moment arises, which is the third call to the body of Christ. Grieving and intercession make us available for the ministry of mercy and comfort.[100]

---

[100] "In The Valley of The Shadow: A September 11, 2001 Reflection" by Rev. Ken Sehested and Rev. Kyle Childress of the Baptist Peace

Holy grief and intercession.

When we grieve over the suffering of our Iraqi brethren, however, we must not "grieve like the rest of men, who have no hope."[101]

Iraq's hope is there for all to see, blazing in the sanctuaries of congregations throughout the nation. Christian families who remain in Iraq, despite the brutal persecution—homes, churches, and businesses bombed and burned, joblessness, fathers and sons murdered, wives and daughters raped, kidnapped, or forcibly married to Muslims.

In the same breath that they pray for protection and provision, they pray as the first century saints prayed, "Now, Lord, consider their threats and enable your servants to speak your word with great boldness."[102]

They are the postscript to Hebrews 11, of whom the world is not worthy.

When we intercede, we should begin by praying for unity, as Jesus did just before he went to the cross.

Jesus was a man who was about to die and knew it. the words of his prayer were among his last words on earth and therefore very important to us.

Additional weight is given to these words because he repeated them. Three times in a single prayer, Jesus interceded for unity in the body of Christ.

Fellowship of North America, October 2001, http://www.bpfna.org/shadow.html.

[101] 1 Thessalonians 4:13

[102] Acts 4:29

> "Holy Father, protect them by the power of your name—the name you gave me—*so that they may be one as we are one*."[103]

> "My prayer is not for them alone. I pray also for those who will believe me through their message, *that all of them may be one*, Father, just as you are in me and I am in you. May they also be in us *so that the world may believe that you have sent me*."[104]

> I have given them the glory that you gave me, *that they may be one as we are one: I in them and you in me.* May they be brought to complete unity *to let the world know that you sent me and have loved them even as you have loved me*."[105]

Why is our unity so important to Jesus? So that the world may believe that God sent him and to let the world know that God loves them just as he loves his Son.

Contrariwise, our disunity declares just as loudly to the world that God did not send Jesus and that he does not love the world just as he loves his Son.

Because the Father will deny his Son nothing, we can say *amen* to Jesus' prayer, confident that unity of the body of Christ is the

---

[103] John 17:11, italics mine.
[104] Ibid, 20-21.
[105] Ibid, 22-23.

Father's will and that he will accomplish what we ask.

In addition to prayer and intercession, we should be open to helping the church in Iraq with material or in-kind support as the Holy Spirit leads us.

Through missions and ministries working in the region, we can become sister churches to Iraqi congregations, send short-term missionaries, and provide other assistance.

In the meantime, we can support those missions and ministries by filling their hands with Bibles, food, clothing, and medicine, and help them meet other essential needs of the brethren, as well as enabling Iraqi congregations to help and bless their Muslim neighbors.

As we bless our brothers and sisters, we become partners with God as he fulfills his promise to bless the nations through Iraq, his amazing handiwork.

Appendix I

Life in Ancient Baghdad

In the 600s A.D., nomadic peoples from the Arabian Peninsula became Muslims. Within a hundred years, Muslims forged an empire that dominated Persia, northern Egypt and the Arab Peninsula. As the empire grew, various clans and dynasties claimed the throne.

In 762, the second Abbasid caliph, al-Mansur, moved the empire's capital from Damascus to a tiny Persian village named Baghdad. Four years later, 100,000 artisans, architects, carpenters and other laborers completed the spectacular new capital.

Baghdad became known across the empire as the Round City because of the walls that encircled it. A smooth outer wall, topped with many watchtowers, protected mud-brick houses, mosques, and suqs (marketplaces). A second wall ringed the city's center. Nearly 100 feet tall, this massive wall was 145 feet thick at its base and 40 feet thick at the top. A third inner wall with an enormous golden gate protected the palace where the caliph lived with his wives, children, slaves and bodyguards.

Soon suburbs bursting with houses, mosques, shops, bathhouses, and suqs spread across the banks of the Tigris. Within a few decades, Baghdad blossomed into a center of international trade, political might, and cultural influence. Only a hundred years after its founding, the city population hovered at one million people.

Many villagers living near Baghdad were *dhimmis* (non-Muslims, including Christians, Jews and Zoroastrians). Caliphs allowed dhimmis to practice their own religions. But dhimmis also had to pay a special tax. Some caliphs imposed other rules on the dhimmis. In 850 A.D. Caliph al-Mutawakkil made Jews and Christians wear yellow coats and attach balls to the saddles of their mules or donkeys. In addition, Muslim jurors couldn't accept a non-Muslim's word over that of a Muslim. Despite the restrictions, many dhimmis prospered. By the late ninth century, some Christians had become viziers (the caliph's right-hand men), and Jews had held high government offices.

When Muslim forces defeated a Chinese army in 751, Chinese prisoners taught their captors how to make paper. By 794, Baghdad had its first paper mill. By the tenth century, Baghdad's suqs boasted as many as a hundred bookshops. Baghdad was home to one of Islam's greatest libraries – the House of Wisdom, established in 830 by Caliph al-Ma'mun. Persian and Indian teachings were translated into Arabic. Baghdad's scholars also translated Greek treatises on mathematics, astronomy, medicine, and philosophy.

But not all books in Baghdad were for learning. One of Baghdad's most famous story collections, *One Thousand and One Nights*, was translated into Arabic in the tenth century. Some of the well-known stories include Aladdin, Ali Baba, and Sinbad the Sailor.[106]

---

[106] Excerpted by permission from Daily Life in Ancient and Modern Baghdad, Dawn Kotapish, ©2000 Runestone Press/Minneapolis, A Division of Lerner Publishing Group. 241 First Avenue North, Minneapolis, Minnesota 55401, ISBN 0 8225 3219 0.

Appendix II

WARNING!

The following report by the U. S. Department of State contains graphic descriptions of physical human rights violations which may be offensive to some readers.

Country Reports on Human Rights Practices - 2001

Released by the Bureau of Democracy, Human Rights, and Labor
March 4, 2002

[This report has been edited for space – the authors]

[Secretary Colin L. Powell held a special briefing to announce the release of the 2001 Human Rights Reports. Assistant Secretary for the Bureau of Democracy, Human Rights, and Labor, Lorne W. Craner, also spoke and held a Question and Answer session.

The report entitled "Country Reports on Human Rights Practices" is submitted to the Congress by the Department of State in compliance with sections 116(d) and 502(b) of the Foreign Assistance Act of 1961 (FAA), as amended, and section 504 of the Trade Act of 1974, as amended. The law provides that the Secretary of State shall transmit to the Speaker of the House of Representatives and the Committee on Foreign Relations of the Senate, by February 25 "a full and complete report regarding the status of internationally recognized human rights, within the meaning of subsection (A) in countries that receive assistance under this part, and (B) in all other foreign countries which are members of the United Nations and which are not otherwise the subject of a human rights report under this Act."]

Political power in Iraq[1] lies exclusively in a repressive one-party apparatus dominated by Saddam Hussein and members of his extended family. The provisional Constitution of 1968 stipulates that the Arab Ba'th Socialist Party governs Iraq through the Revolutionary Command Council (RCC), which exercises both executive and legislative authority. President Saddam Hussein, who also is Prime Minister, Chairman of the RCC, and Secretary General of the Regional Command of the Ba'th Party, wields decisive power. Hussein and his Government continued to refer to an October 1995 non-democratic "referendum" on his presidency, in which he received 99.96 percent of the vote. This referendum included neither secret ballots nor opposing candidates, and many credible reports indicated that voters feared possible reprisal for a dissenting vote. Ethnically and linguistically the Iraqi population includes Arabs, Kurds, Turkmens, Assyrians, Yazidis, and Armenians. The religious mix likewise is varied and consists of Shi'a and Sunni Muslims (both Arab and Kurdish), Christians (including Chaldeans and Assyrians), and a small number of Jews and Mandaeans. Civil uprisings have occurred in previous years, especially in the north and the south. The Government has reacted with extreme repression against those who oppose or even question it. The judiciary is not independent, and the President may override any court decision.

The Government's security apparatus includes militias attached to the President, the Ba'th Party, and the Interior Ministry. Military and paramilitary forces often fulfill an internal security role. The military and security forces play a central role in maintaining the environment of intimidation and fear on which government power rests. The Government makes no attempt to acknowledge, investigate, or punish officials or members of the military or security forces accused of human rights abuses. Military and security forces committed widespread, serious, and systematic human rights abuses.

The Government's human rights record remained extremely poor. Citizens do not have the right to change their government. The Government continued to execute summarily alleged political opponents and leaders in the Shi'a religious community. Reports suggest that persons were executed merely because of their association with an opposition group or as part of a continuing effort to reduce prison populations. The Government continued to be responsible for disappearances and to kill and torture persons suspected of--or related to persons suspected of--economic crimes, military desertion, and a variety of other activities. Security forces routinely tortured, beat, raped, and otherwise abused detainees. Prison conditions are extremely poor and at times life threatening. The Government reportedly has conducted "prison cleansing" campaigns to kill inmates in order to relieve overcrowding in the prisons. The authorities routinely used arbitrary arrest and detention, prolonged detention, and incommunicado detention, and continued to deny citizens the basic right to due process. Saddam Hussein and his inner circle of supporters continued to impose arbitrary rule. The Government continued to infringe on citizens' privacy rights.

The Government restricts severely freedoms of speech, the press, assembly, association, religion, and movement. The U.N. Special Rapporteur on the situation of human rights in the country issued a report in January detailing ongoing, grievous violations of human rights by the Government. The

U.N. Commission on Human Rights and the U.N. General Assembly passed resolutions in April and November criticizing the Government's suppression of these freedoms. Human rights abuses remain difficult to document because of the Government's efforts to conceal the facts, including its prohibition on the establishment of independent human rights organizations, its persistent refusal to grant visits to human rights monitors, and its continued restrictions designed to prevent dissent. Denied entry to the country, the Special Rapporteur bases his reports on the Government's human rights abuses on interviews with recent emigrants, interviews with opposition groups and others that have contacts inside the country, and on published reports from outside the country. Violence and discrimination against women occur. The Government has enacted laws affording a variety of protections to women; however, it is difficult to determine the practical effects of such protections. The Government neglects the health and nutritional needs of children, and discriminates against religious minorities and ethnic groups. The Government restricts severely trade union rights. Child labor persists, and there were instances of forced labor.

RESPECT FOR HUMAN RIGHTS

Section 1 Respect for the Integrity of the Person, Including Freedom From:

a. Arbitrary or Unlawful Deprivation of Life

The Government committed numerous political and other extrajudicial killings. The Government has a long record of executing perceived or alleged opponents. In a report released by the U.N. Secretary General on September 13, the U.N. Special Rapporteur criticized the Government for the "sheer number of executions" taking place in the country, the number of “extrajudicial executions on political grounds,” and “the absence of a due process of the law.” The list of offenses requiring a mandatory death penalty has grown substantially in the past few years and now includes anything that could be characterized as “sabotaging the national economy,” including forgery, as well as smuggling cars, spare parts, material, heavy equipment, and machinery. The Special Rapporteur has noted that membership in certain political parties is punishable by death, that there is a pervasive fear of death for any act or expression of dissent, and that there are recurrent reports of the use of the death penalty for such offenses as “insulting” the President or the Ba’th Party. “The mere suggestion that someone is not a supporter of the President carries the prospect of the death penalty,” the Special Rapporteur stated. The Government made no attempt to answer allegations of either past or present political or extrajudicial killings, investigate such abuses, nor identify and punish the perpetrators.

In a report released in January, Amnesty International reported that in October 2000 the Government had executed dozens of women accused of prostitution.

In February the Government reportedly executed 37 political detainees for opposition activity. According to press reports, prominent Kurd writer Muhammad Jamil Bandi Rozhbayani was killed in March after a visit to his home by intelligence service personnel investigating his writings regarding the Government’s Arabization and ethnic cleansing programs. In May the Government reportedly

executed two Shi’a clerics, Abdulsattar Abed-Ibrahim al-Mausawi and Ahmad al-Hashemi, for claiming that the Government was involved in the killing of a Shi'a cleric in 1999 and the killings of four engineers from the Electricity Board for receiving bribes in May (see Section 1.d.). According to credible reporting, in June security forces killed another Shi'a cleric, Hussein Bahar al-Uloom, for refusing to appear on television to congratulate Qusay Saddam Hussein for his election to a Ba'th Party position.

Such killings continue an apparent government policy of eliminating prominent Shi'a clerics who are suspected of disloyalty to the Government. In 1998 and 1999, the Government killed a number of leading Shi'a clerics, prompting the former Special Rapporteur in 1999 to express his concern to the Government that the killings might be part of a systematic attack by government officials on the independent leadership of the Shi'a Muslim community (see Section 2.c.). The Government did not respond to the Special Rapporteur's letter.

In September the Government executed 28 political prisoners in Abu Ghurayb prison as a part of its "prison cleansing" campaign. During 2000 the Special Rapporteur received reports referring to a "prison cleansing" execution campaign taking place in Abu Ghurayb, Radwaniyah, and other prisons. Opposition groups, including the Supreme Council for the Islamic Revolution in Iraq (SCIRI), the Iraqi Communist Party (ICP), the Iraqi National Congress (INC), and others with a network inside the country, provided detailed accounts of summary executions, including the names of hundreds of persons killed. A former officer from the Mukhabarat (Intelligence Service) reported that he participated in a 1998 mass murder at Abu Ghurayb prison following a Revolutionary Command Council directive to "clean out" the country's prisons. The Government's motive for such high numbers of summary executions--estimated at more than 3,000 since 1997--may be linked to reported intimidation of the population and reduction of prison populations. The Government has made no effort to investigate current or past cases, answer accusations about the executions, or identify and punish the perpetrators.

Government agents targeted for killing family members of defectors (see Section 1.f.). For example, in May the Government reportedly tortured to death the mother of three Iraqi defectors for her children's opposition activities. In October 2000, security forces reportedly beheaded a number of women suspected of prostitution and some men suspected of facilitating or covering up such activities (see Section 5). Security agents reportedly decapitated numerous women and men in front of their family members. According to Amnesty International (AI), the victim's heads were displayed in front of their homes for several days. Thirty of the victims' names reportedly were published, which included three doctors and one medical assistant.

Reports of deaths due to poor prison conditions continued (see Section 1.c.).

Many persons who were displaced forcibly still lived in tent camps under harsh conditions, which also resulted in many deaths (see Sections 2.d. and 5).

As in previous years, the Government continued to deny the widespread killings of Kurds in the north of the country during the "Anfal" Campaign of 1988 (see Sections 1.b. and 1.g.). Both the Special

Rapporteur and Human Rights Watch (HRW) have concluded that the Government's policies against the Kurds raise questions of crimes against humanity and violations of the 1948 Genocide Convention.

b. Disappearance

There continued to be widespread reports of widespread disappearances. The Government continued to ignore the more than 16,000 cases conveyed to it in 1994 and 1995 by the U.N., as well as requests from the Governments of Kuwait and Saudi Arabia to account for the whereabouts of those who had disappeared during Iraq's 1990-91 occupation of Kuwait, and from Iran regarding the whereabouts of prisoners of war that Iraq captured in the 1980-88 Iran-Iraq war. The majority of the 16,496 cases known to the Special Rapporteur are persons of Kurdish origin who disappeared during the 1988 Anfal Campaign. The Special Rapporteur estimated that the total number of Kurds who disappeared during that period could reach several tens of thousands. Human Rights Watch (HRW) estimated the total at between 70,000 and 150,000, and AI at more than 100,000. The second largest group of cases known to the Special Rapporteur consists of Shi'a Muslims who were reported to have disappeared in the late 1970's and early 1980's as their families were expelled to Iran due to their alleged Persian ancestry.

The Government failed to return, or account for, a large number of Kuwaiti citizens and citizens of other countries who were detained during the Iraqi occupation of Kuwait and continues to refuse to cooperate with the Tripartite Commission to resolve the cases. Of 609 cases of missing Kuwaiti citizens under review by the Tripartite Commission on Gulf War Missing, only 3 have been resolved. Iran reports that the Government still has not accounted for 5,000 Iranian prisoners of war (POW's) missing since the Iran-Iraq War.

c. Torture and Other Cruel, Inhuman, or Degrading Treatment or Punishment

The Constitution prohibits torture; however, the security services routinely and systematically tortured detainees. According to former prisoners, torture techniques included branding, electric shocks administered to the genitals and other areas, beating, pulling out of fingernails, burning with hot irons and blowtorches, suspension from rotating ceiling fans, dripping acid on the skin, rape, breaking of limbs, denial of food and water, extended solitary confinement in dark and extremely small compartments, and threats to rape or otherwise harm family members and relatives. Evidence of such torture often was apparent when security forces returned the mutilated bodies of torture victims to their families. There were persistent reports that the families were made to pay for the cost of executions. Refugees who arrived in Europe often reported instances of torture to receiving governments, and displayed scars and mutilations to substantiate their claims.

For some years, the Special Rapporteur has expressed concern about cruel and unusual punishments prescribed by the law, including amputations and brandings.

Human rights organizations and opposition groups continued to receive reports of women who suffered from severe psychological trauma after being raped while in custody. Security forces also reportedly sexually assaulted both government officials and opposition members in order to blackmail them into compliance.

The security forces allegedly raped women who were captured during the Anfal Campaign and during the occupation of Kuwait. The Government never has acknowledged these reports, conducted any investigation, nor taken action against those who committed the rapes.

Prison conditions are extremely poor and life threatening. Overcrowding is a serious problem. In May 1998, Labor and Social Affairs Minister Abdul Hamid Aziz Sabah stated in an interview that "the prisons are filled to five times their capacity and the situation is serious." Certain prisons are infamous for routine mistreatment of detainees and prisoners. Abu Ghurayb, Baladiat, Makasib, Rashidiya, Radwaniyah, and other prisons reportedly have torture chambers. The Al-Radwaniyah detention center is a former POW facility near Baghdad and reportedly the site of torture as well as mass executions (see Section 1.a.).

In 2000 the Special Rapporteur reported receiving information about two detention facilities in which prisoners are locked in metal boxes the size of coffins that reportedly are opened for only 30 minutes each day. A multistory underground detention and torture center reportedly was built under the general military hospital building close to the Al-Rashid military camp on the outskirts of Baghdad.

d. Arbitrary Arrest, Detention, or Exile

The Constitution and the Legal Code explicitly prohibit arbitrary arrest and detention; however, the authorities routinely engaged in these practices. The Special Rapporteur continued to receive reports of widespread arbitrary arrest and detention, often for long periods of time, without access to a lawyer or the courts. As indicated in the November 1999 AI report, "Iraq: Victims of Systematic Repression," many thousands of persons have been arrested arbitrarily in the last few years because of suspected opposition activities or because they were related to persons sought by the authorities. Those arrested often were taken away by plainclothes security agents, who offered no explanation and produced no warrant to the person or family members (see Section 1.f.). The authorities deny detainees legal representation and visits by family members. In most cases, family members do not know the whereabouts of detainees and do not make inquiries due to fear of reprisal. Many persons are taken away in front of family members, who hear nothing further until days, months, or years later, when they are told to retrieve the often-mutilated corpse of their relative.

Mass arbitrary arrests and detentions often occurred in areas in which antigovernment leaflets were distributed. In June the Coalition for Justice in Iraq reported that the Government arrested dozens of lawyers and jurists for distributing antigovernment leaflets. The leaflets reportedly indicated the authors' intent to expose the Government's violations of human rights. Security forces arrested hundreds of persons in al-Najaf, Karbala, and the Shi'a section of Baghdad following an anonymous distribution of antigovernment leaflets in 2000. Other arrests have no apparent basis.

The Government reportedly targeted the Shi'a Muslim community for arbitrary arrest and other abuses. For example, in May the Government reportedly executed two Shi'a clerics, Abdulsattar Abed-Ibrahim al-Mausawi and Ahmad al-Hashemi, for claiming that the Government was involved in the killing of a Shi'a cleric in 1999 and the killings of four engineers from the Electricity Board for receiving bribes. In the weeks preceding the

February 1999 killing of Ayatollah Sadeq Al-Sadr and two of his sons, many of Al-Sadr's aides were arrested, and their whereabouts still were unknown at year's end (see Sections 1.a., 1.b., and 1.g.). Hundreds more reportedly were arrested and the houses of many demolished in the weeks following the killing (see Section 1.g.).

Hundreds of Fayli (Shi'a) Kurds and other citizens of Iranian origin, who had disappeared in the early 1980's during the Iran-Iraq war, reportedly were being held incommunicado at the Abu Ghurayb prison. According to a report received by the Special Rapporteur in 1998, such persons have been detained without charge for close to 2 decades in extremely harsh conditions. The report states that many of the detainees were used as subjects in the country's outlawed experimental chemical and biological weapons programs.

Although no statistics were available, observers estimated the number of political detainees to be in the tens of thousands, some of whom have been held for decades.

The Government announced in June 1999 a general amnesty for citizens who had left the country illegally or were exiled officially for a specified period of time but failed to return after the period of

exile expired (see Section 2.d.). No citizens are known to have returned to the country based upon this amnesty. An estimated 1 to 2 million self-exiled citizens reportedly remain fearful of returning to the country.

e. Denial of Fair Public Trial

The judiciary is not independent, and there is no check on the President's power to override any court decision. In 1999 the Special Rapporteur and international human rights groups observed that the repressive nature of the political and legal systems precludes the rule of law. Numerous laws facilitate continued repression, and the Government uses extrajudicial methods to extract confessions or coerce cooperation.

There are two parallel judicial systems: the regular courts, which try common criminal offenses; and the special security courts, which generally try national security cases but also may try criminal cases. In addition to the Court of Appeal, there is the Court of Cassation, which is the highest court.

Special security courts have jurisdiction in all cases involving espionage and treason, peaceful political dissent, smuggling, currency exchange violations, and drug trafficking. According to the Special Rapporteur and other sources, military officers or civil servants with no legal training head these tribunals, which hear cases in secret. Authorities often hold defendants incommunicado and do not permit contact with lawyers (see Section 1.d.). The courts admit confessions extracted by torture, which often served as the basis for conviction (see Section 1.c.). Many cases appear to end in summary execution, although defendants may appeal to the President for clemency. Saddam Hussein may grant clemency in any case that suits his political goals or personal predilection.

The Government shields certain groups from prosecution for alleged crimes. For example, a 1990 decree grants immunity to men who commit "honor crimes," a violent assault with intent to commit murder against a women by a relative for her perceived immodest behavior or alleged sexual misconduct (see Section 5). A 1992 decree grants immunity from prosecution to members of the Ba'th Party and security forces who killed anyone while in pursuit of army deserters.

It was difficult to estimate the number of political prisoners, because the Government rarely acknowledges arrests or imprisonments, and families are afraid to talk about arrests. Many of the tens of thousands of persons who disappeared or were killed in the past few years originally were held as political prisoners.

f. Arbitrary Interference With Privacy, Family, Home, or Correspondence

The Government routinely ignored constitutional provisions designed to protect the confidentiality of mail, telegraphic correspondence, and telephone conversations. The Government periodically jammed news broadcasts from outside the country, including those of opposition groups (see Section 2.a.). The security services and the Ba'th Party maintain pervasive networks of informers to deter dissident activity and instill fear in the public.

The authorities continued systematically to detain, abuse, and kill family members and close associates of alleged government opponents (see Sections 1.a., 1.b., 1.d., and 1.g.). In June 2000, a former general reportedly received a videotape of security forces raping a female family member. He subsequently received a telephone call from an intelligence agent who stated that another female relative was being held and warned him to stop speaking out against the Government.

The Government continues its Arabization campaign of ethnic cleansing designed to harass and expel ethnic Kurds and Turkmen from government-controlled areas. According to press reports and opposition sources, the Government has displaced forcibly hundreds of families. As in previous years, the regime periodically sealed off entire districts in Kirkuk and conducted day-long, house-to-house searches (see Sections 2.d. and 5). Government officials also took hostage members of minority groups to intimidate their families into leaving their home regions (see Sections 1.d., 2.d., and 5).

In the past, the authorities demolished the houses and detained and executed family members of Shi'a who protested government actions (see Section 1.g.).

g. Use of Excessive Force and Violations of Humanitarian Law In Internal Conflicts

The Government continued to "Arabize" certain Kurdish areas, such as the urban centers of Kirkuk and Mosul, through the forced movement of local residents from their homes and villages and their replacement by Arabs from outside the area (see Sections 2.d. and 5).

Landmines in the north, mostly planted by the Government before 1991, continued to kill and maim civilians. Many of the mines were laid during the Iran-Iraq and Gulf Wars; however, the army failed to clear them before it abandoned the area. Landmines also are a problem along the Iraq-Iran border throughout the central and southern areas in the country. There is no information regarding civilian casualties or the Government's efforts, if any, to clear old mine fields in areas under the central Government's control. According to reports by the U.N. Office of Project Services, the Mines

Advisory Group, and Norwegian Peoples' Aid, landmines have killed more than 3,000 persons in the three northern governates since the 1991 uprising.

In December 1998, the Government declared that mine-clearing activity was subversive and ordered NGO workers performing such activity to leave the country.

In 2000 authorities continued to target alleged supporters of Al-Sadr. In February 2000, security officials reportedly executed 30 religious school students who had been arrested after Al-Sadr's killing. In March 2000, numerous Shi'a who fled the country in 1999 and 2000, told HRW that security forces interrogated, detained, and tortured them. In May 2000, six additional students who were arrested following the killing were sentenced to death.

After the 1991 Gulf War, victims and eyewitnesses described war crimes perpetrated by the Government, including deliberate killing, torture, rape, pillage, and hostage-taking. HRW and other organizations have worked with various governments to bring a genocide case at the International Court of Justice against the Government for its conduct of the Anfal campaign against the Kurds in 1988.

Section 2 Respect for Civil Liberties, Including:

a. Freedom of Speech and Press

The Special Rapporteur stated in October 1999 that citizens lived "in a climate of fear," in which whatever they said or did, particularly in the area of politics, involved "the risk of arrest and interrogation by the police or military intelligence."

He noted that "the mere suggestion that someone is not a supporter of the President carries the prospect of the death penalty." In June the Human Rights Alliance reported that the Government had killed more than 500 journalists and other intellectuals in the past decade.

The Government regularly jams foreign news broadcasts (see Section 1.f.). Satellite dishes, modems, and fax machines are banned, although some restrictions reportedly were lifted in 1999. Government-controlled areas have only two terrestrial television channels, the official Iraq Television and Youth TV, owned by Uday Saddam Hussein. The Information Ministry announced a plan to make limited satellite television service available, offering eight channels at a cost of $33 to $38 (10,000 to 12,000 dinars) per month, twice the average wage of a government employee. In September Uday Hussein reportedly had assumed control of the satellite television service.

c. Freedom of Religion

The Ministry of Endowments and Religious Affairs monitors places of worship, appoints the clergy, approves the building and repair of all places of worship, and approves the publication of all religious literature.

The Government has for decades conducted a brutal campaign of murder, summary execution, and protracted arbitrary arrest against the religious leaders and followers of the majority Shi'a Muslim population (See Sections 1.a., 1.d., and 1.g.). Despite nominal legal protection of religious equality, the Government has repressed severely the Shi'a clergy and those who follow the Shi'a faith. Forces from the Mukhabarat, General Security (Amn Al-Amm), the Military Bureau, Saddam's Commandos (Fedayeen Saddam), and the Ba'th Party have killed senior Shi'a clerics, desecrated Shi'a mosques and holy sites, and interfered with Shi'a religious education. Security agents reportedly are stationed at all the major Shi'a mosques and shrines and search, harass, and arbitrarily arrest worshipers.

The following government restrictions on religious rights remained in effect during the year: Restrictions and outright bans on communal Friday prayer by Shi'a Muslims; restrictions on the loaning of books by Shi'a mosque libraries; a ban on the broadcast of Shi'a programs on government-controlled radio or television; a ban on the publication of Shi'a books, including prayer books and guides; a ban on funeral processions other than those organized by the Government; a ban on other Shi'a funeral observances such as gatherings for Koran reading; and the prohibition of certain processions and public meetings that commemorate Shi'a holy days. Shi'a groups report that they captured documents from the security services during the 1991 uprising that listed thousands of forbidden Shi'a religious writings.

The Government also has sought to undermine the identity of minority Christian (Assyrian and Chaldean) and Yazidi groups.

The Special Rapporteur and others reported that the Government has engaged in various abuses against the country's 350,000 Assyrian and Chaldean Christians, especially in terms of forced movements from northern areas and repression of political rights (see Section 2.d.). Most Assyrians live in the northern governates, and the Government often has accused them of collaborating with Iraqi Kurds. In the north, Kurdish groups often refer to Assyrians as

Kurdish Christians. Military forces destroyed numerous Assyrian churches during the 1988 Anfal Campaign and reportedly tortured and executed many Assyrians. Both major Kurdish political parties have indicated that the Government occasionally targets Assyrians, as well as ethnic Kurds and Turkmens, in expulsions from Kirkuk in order to attempt to Arabize the city (see Section 2.d.).

d. Freedom of Movement Within the Country, Foreign Travel, Emigration, and Repatriation

The Government restricts movement within the country of citizens and foreigners. Police checkpoints are common on major roads and highways. Persons who enter sensitive border areas and numerous designated security zones are subject to arrest.

The Government requires citizens to obtain specific government authorization and expensive exit visas for foreign travel. Citizens may not make more than two trips abroad annually. Before traveling abroad, citizens are required to post collateral, which is refundable only upon their return. There are restrictions on the amount of currency that may be taken out of the country. Women are not permitted to travel outside the country alone; male relatives must escort them (see Section 5). Prior to December 1999, every student who wished to travel abroad was required to provide a guarantor who would be liable if the student failed to return. In December 1999, authorities banned all travel for students (including those in grade school), canceled spring and summer holidays, and enrolled students in compulsory military training and weapons-use courses.

Non-Arab citizens are forced to either change their ethnicity on their identity documents and adopt Arabic names or be expelled to the Kurd-controlled northern governates. Persons may avoid expulsion if they relinquish their Kurdish, Turkmen, or Assyrian identity and register as Arabs. Persons who refuse to relinquish their identity may have their assets expropriated and their ration cards withdrawn prior to being deported.

Authorities estimate that since 1991, more than 100,000 persons have been displaced as part of the Arabization program.

According to numerous deportees in the north, the Government generally uses a systematic procedure to evict and deport non-Arab citizens. Frequently, a security force official demands that a family change its ethnicity from Kurdish or Turkmen to Arab. Subsequently, security officials frequently arrest the head of household and inform the other family members that the person will be imprisoned until they agree to settle elsewhere in the country. Such families frequently choose to move to the north; family members must sign a form that states that the departure is voluntary and they are not allowed to take any property or their food ration cards issued under the U.N. oil-for-food program. The Government frequently transfers the families' houses to Arab Ba'th Party members.

Those expelled are not permitted to return. The Special Rapporteur reported in 1999 that citizens who provide employment, food, or shelter to returning or newly arriving Kurds are subject to arrest. The Government denies that it expels non-Arab families.

Section 3 Respect for Political Rights: The Right of Citizens to Change Their Government

Citizens do not have the right to change their government. The President wields power over all instruments of government. Most important officials either are members of Saddam Hussein's family or are family allies from his hometown of Tikrit. Although the Government has taken steps to increase the perception of democracy, the political process still is controlled firmly by the State. The 1995 so-called referendum on Saddam Hussein's presidency was not free and was dismissed as a sham by most international observers. It included neither voter privacy nor opposing candidates, and many credible reports indicated that voters feared possible reprisal if they cast a dissenting vote. A total of 500 persons reportedly were arrested in Karbala, Baghdad, and Ramadi provinces for casting negative ballots, and a member of the intelligence services reportedly was executed for refusing to vote for the President.

As in previous years, the Government did not allow the U.N. Special Rapporteur to visit the country, nor did it respond to his requests for information.

[1] The United States does not have diplomatic representation in Iraq. This report draws to a large extent on non-U.S. Government sources.

Appendix III

The Mission of Manara Book Ministries

Manara is the Arabic word for Lighthouse. In 1978, Isam Ghattas and his wife, Nihad, opened Manara Bookshop in Amman. Since then, they have taken Bibles, textbooks and other literature to book fairs and exhibitions throughout Jordan and the surrounding Gulf countries. They opened Camp Gilead – a summer children's camp – in 1987. Five years later more than 1,000 children from Jordan and Iraq attended, and more than 100 came to faith in Christ.

Following the first Gulf War, Manara Book Ministries began to minister to Kuwaiti refugees. These families joined countless Palestinian, Iraqi and Sudanese refugees in the largest refugee population on earth. And Manara Development Ministries was born. This includes two daycare centers for low-income families – the only daycare centers in Jordan – and an embroidery cottage industry called Mercy Ministries. Manara also distributes vital food and clothing to needy Christian families in Jordan and Iraq.

Today, Manara Bookshop is the only Christian bookstore in Jordan. It is the heart of Manara Book Ministries, which extends to Jordan's 7,000 prison inmates – both Muslim and Christian – and into many other countries, including Syria, Yeman, Lebanon and Iraq.

In Iraq, after seven years of supplying the church with more than one million Bibles and other Christian literature and audio and video cassettes, Manara began a relief effort for 2,500 of the poorest Christian families in Baghdad and another 2,500 in Mosul. And the ministry recently opened a huge Manara Bookshop and Internet Café in the heart of Baghdad.

Because of its success, Manara and its staff members have suffered attacks from Muslim extremists, as described in the following news report:

Gaza's Christian bookseller killed

By Eric Silver

JERUSALEM, Monday 08 October 2007 (*The Independent*)— The manager of Gaza's only Christian bookshop, who was abducted on Saturday by suspected Muslim extremists, was found dead yesterday. Medical officials said Rami Ayyad, 31, had been shot and stabbed. He was the father of two small children and his wife is pregnant with their third.

He is reported to have received several death threats since his Protestant bible shop was fire bombed six months ago, destroying shelves of books and pamphlets. He told friends that bearded men in a car stalked him and looked at him strangely after he locked up on Thursday.

The killers seized him as he left the shop on Saturday night. Suhad Massad, the director of the local Baptist bible society which runs the shop, said friends called his mobile phone when he did not arrive home. He told them he was running late.

Mr Ayyad's mother, Anisa, said he phoned his family. "He said he was going to be with the 'people' for another two hours and that if he was not back by then, he would not be returning for a long, long time." She added that Mr Ayyad, who was born into a Greek Orthodox family but worshipped in a Baptist congregation, had "redeemed Christ with his blood".

About 3,000 Arab Christians live among 1.4 million Muslims in the Gaza Strip. Attacks on Christians and their property are rare, but more than 40 video cassette shops and internet cafes, identified with Western values, have been bombed in the past year. So was an American school. A shadowy group calling itself the Righteous Swords of Islam claimed responsibility. Up to 300 Muslims and Christians attended a memorial service for Mr Ayyad in a Greek Orthodox church in Gaza City yesterday. The mourners were reluctant to point fingers or to open a rift between the faiths.

Ms Massad said: "We don't know who was behind the killing or why. Was it for money, or was it because he was selling Bibles?" Describing him as a man with a warm heart, a smiling face and no enemies. "We try to show Jesus' love for all people, but without evangelism."

Raji Sourani, director of the Palestinian Centre for Human Rights, maintained: "This ugly act has no support by any religious group here." Nicholas Issa, a 50-year-old Christian, said: "Today is a black day for Gaza. We hope he was not killed because he was a Christian."

Another Christian, Jan Sa'ad, 42, said: "This has never happened before in Gaza. If somebody thinks this murder will make Christians leave, they are mistaken. This is our homeland. We are as patriotic as anyone."

About the authors

Isam Ghattas, founder and director of Manara International, and his wife, Nihad, have ministered to the persecuted church and spread the Gospel throughout the Middle East since 1968. Despite attacks and death threats, Isam and his staff distribute bibles and other Christian literature through book fairs and Manara Bookshop in Amman, Jordan; provide humanitarian aid to refugees and persecuted Christians in Jordan, Lebanon, Syria, and Iraq; minister to Jordanian and refugee children in two Manara preschools; and share the light of the Gospel to nearly a thousand youth every summer at Camp Gilead.

The author of the international bestseller, *Son of Hamas*, Ron Brackin has traveled extensively in the Middle East as an investigative journalist. He was in the West Bank and Gaza during the Al-Aqsa Intifada, on assignment in Baghdad and Mosul after the fall of Iraq and more recently with the rebels and refugees of Southern Sudan and Darfur. He has contributed articles and columns to many publications, including *USA Today* and *The Washington Times* and is the author of other fiction and nonfiction books. He was a broadcast journalist with WTOP-AM, Post-Newsweek's all-news radio station in Washington D.C. and weekend news anchor on Metromedia's WASH-FM. And he served as a congressional press secretary under the Reagan Administration. Visit his website at www.ronbrackin.com.

Other Books by Ron Brackin

The eldest son of Sheikh Hassan Yousef, a founder of the terrorist organization Hamas, Mosab Hassan Yousef was groomed from birth to replace his father. As a teenager, imprisoned and tortured by the Israelis, Mosab saw how Hamas abused and tortured its own, forcing him to ask himself, "Who is my enemy?" The quest to find the answer led him from Islam to Christianity—and from Hamas to serving for ten years as a double-agent for the Shin Bet, Israel's internal security forces, during which time he saved countless Israeli, Palestinian, and American lives and put countless terrorists behind bars…including his father!

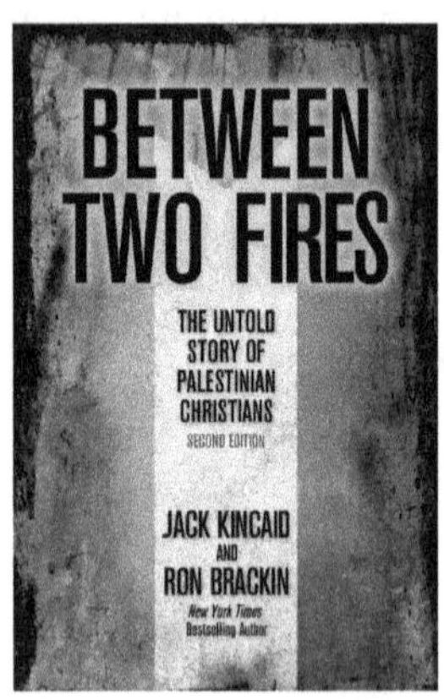

The minority of minorities, Palestinian Evangelicals tell their amazing—often tragic—stories in *Between Two Fires*. Inspiring accounts of faith and courage mingle with brutal testimonies of frustration and fear. Who is right? Whose side is God on? How should Christians respond?

In a world plagued by terrorism and anarchy and staggering on the brink of global economic collapse, arises a young man out of Lebanon, with extraordinary powers and the mission to lead the world back to the Garden of Eden. With the hope of immortality, the world's finest scientific and theological minds find the location of the Tree of Life, underneath 6,000 years of civilization—but one nation blocks the way.

Before 221 b Baker Street, young Sherlock Holmes lodged in his rooms at Oxford. Before Dr. John H. Watson, Holmes was accompanied by his college don, Rev. Charles Dodgson, aka Lewis Carroll. Be prepared to enter the dark underworld of Victorian London! Seven Dials, Billingsgate, and the waterfront. A world peopled with murderers and magicians, royalty and rogues.

The entire text of Bram Stoker's timeless horror classic with a bible study at the end of each chapter. While Jesus taught about the kingdom of God using the farms, fields, and waters of Galilee, Ron Brackin gleans from the dark forests and mountainous wilds of Transylvania.

Encouraged by his pastor to share the Lord's Supper more frequently—at home, at work, wherever and whenever—Ron Brackin set out to have an adventure with God. And now, he invites readers to come along on a delightful journey deep into the kingdom of God. But be warned: you may not want to stop at the end of thirty-one days.

The entire text of Charles Dickens's classic story of mystery, mischief, and murder with a bible study at the end of each chapter. While Jesus taught about the kingdom of God using the farms, fields, and waters of Galilee, Ron Brackin gleans from the foul slums and draconian social institutions of 19th century London.

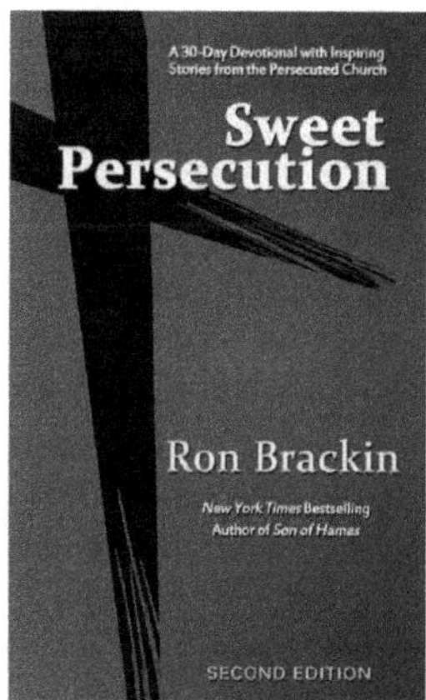

When was the last time you heard a sermon on the theology of suffering? Yet, persecution and suffering are as much a part of the normal Christian life as prayer and worship. This powerful little devotional is filled with true testimonies from the persecuted church that will strengthen, encourage, and inspire you and help you bless others.

Includes the entire original script, with a Bible study at the end of each of the 17 scenes. While Jesus taught about the kingdom of God using the farms, fields, and waters of Galilee, Ron Brackin gleans from the lush gardens and orchards on the 17th century estate of Leonato, governor of the port city of Messina, on Sicily.

Christianity is a roller coaster ride. Whoever says it ain't, don't got a ticket. One day, you're toppling Philistines like ten-pins. Next day, you're hiding in a cave, surrounded by 400 losers. Like David—and every Christian who ever took Jesus for better or worse, richer or poorer, in sickness and in health, Ron Brackin has his ups and downs, expressed herein in 86 bits of verse.

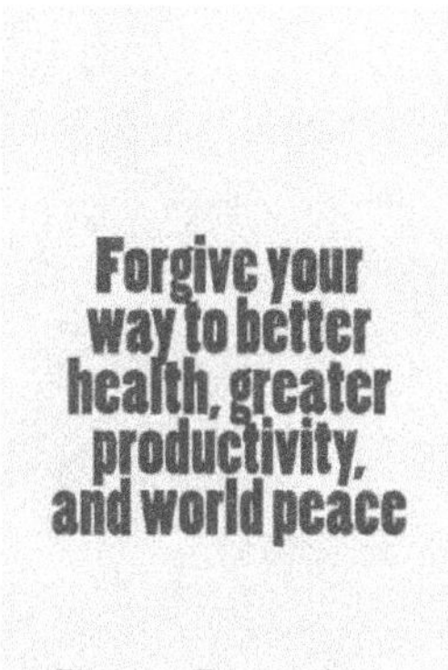

People who forgive live healthier and longer and have better marriages than people who don't. Corporate executives who train their employees to forgive waste less money than those who don't. Nations and ethnic groups that learn to forgive stop trying to destroy one another. So, why do employers still lose billions of dollars to petty squabbles in the workplace? Why are Palestinians and Israelis still killing one another? Why do millions of people still suffer needlessly from stress-related sicknesses and infirmities caused by unforgiveness? Because we lack understanding and courage. The purpose of this little book is to remove one of those obstacles.

Who are you, when you're no longer what you do? The answer for ex-bank executive Ben Waldman awaits him at a Skid Row rescue mission, where his late wife had served as a volunteer. There, he encounters his Virgil, a rabbi-turned-Christian chaplain, and its unpredictable denizens. *The Volunteer*. A screenplay.

www.ingramcontent.com/pod-product-compliance
Lightning Source LLC
Chambersburg PA
CBHW060241050426
42448CB00009B/1541

9780692246443